D1217171

Gateway to the Chinese Classics

A Practical Introduction to Literary Chinese

Gateway
to the
Chinese Classics

A Practical Introduction to Literary Chinese

文言入門

by Jeannette L. Faurot

Copyright © 1995 by Jeannette L. Faurot.

All rights reserved. No part of this book may be used or reproduced in any manner whatsoever without permission in writing from the publisher. Address inquiries to China Books, 2929 24th Street, San Francisco, CA 94110

First Edition 1995

1 3 5 7 9 10 8 6 4 2

Library of Congress Catalog Card Number: 94-074607
ISBN: 0-8351-2537-8

Printed in the United States of America
by China Books & Periodicals.

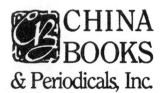

CHINA
BOOKS
& Periodicals, Inc.

Contents

Introduction

What is "Literary Chinese?"

The term *gǔwén* 古文 , literally "ancient writing," may be translated as "Classical Chinese." This is the language of the ancient Chinese historical, philosophical, and poetic texts and their imitations. The term *wényán* 文言 , or "literary language" is a broader term than *gǔwén*, denoting a style of writing characterized by the use of classical particles and syntax, but allowing the use of modern vocabulary. *Wényán* includes Classical Chinese, but also includes modern writings which use classical elements.

Báihuà 白話 , literally "clear speech," refers to the written language that approximates the spoken language in vocabulary and syntax. *Wényán* and *báihuà* may be found in varying proportions in modern texts. *Wényán* is considered to be more formal and often more aesthetically pleasing than *báihuà*, so that modern writing that aspires to weightiness of tone or elegance of expression usually has a relatively high *wényán* content.

Students who wish to read traditional Chinese historical, philosophical or literary works already know that they will need a thorough grounding in *wényán* (or *gǔwén*) to read those texts; but not all students of contemporary Chinese affairs realize the extent to which the literary language permeates the kinds of texts they will encounter in their daily work. Almost any contemporary newspaper or journal article contains literary elements, and many written forms such as newspaper headlines, legal documents, formal invitations, and decorative scrolls, are written in pure *wényán*.

Plan of This Textbook

This textbook is an introduction to *wényán*, and as such it can lead to further study of *gǔwén* classics and/or contemporary texts, depending on the students' interests. Volume 1 focuses on the language of classical texts such as the Confucian *Analects*, *Lao Zi*, early histories and Tang poetry—in other words, on pure Classical Chinese or *gǔwén*. The final lesson in this book also contains an excerpt from the novel *Romance of the Three Kingdoms*, written in an early modern style of *wényán*; it can serve as a bridge to the study of contemporary *wényán*. A second volume, in progress, will be devoted entirely to *wényán* in contemporary Chinese texts.

Lesson 1 of this volume presents some basic structural principles of classical Chinese. Lessons 2-8 introduce basic grammatical particles and the patterns in which they occur, basic classical vocabulary, and selected classical texts. Lessons 9 and 10 contain a selection of well-known classical texts with vocabulary notes. After finishing this textbook, students will have read many of the key works of classical Chinese literature, and should be able to venture into reading other classical texts on their own, with the aid of a good dictionary.

A Word about Grammar

Many scholars have observed that reading *wényán* is more an art than a science, and that it is most effectively learned through experience, with the guidance of a teacher, rather than by attempting to rely solely on mastery of grammatical rules. One problem which troubles almost all beginning students is that the grammar of a given passage is often not immediately apparent, because unlike words in inflected languages, Chinese characters offer no orthographic clues to help readers identify parts of speech or structural function. Grammatical particles, when present, can help specify relations between parts of a sentence, but they are often omitted, especially in poetry and other literary works.

Mastery of basic structural principles and of the use of particles are crucial, and they form the backbone of this book. But students will soon find that even when they thoroughly grasp the grammatical principles and the vocabulary of a given passage, the meaning may still remain opaque. Sometimes the only way to know what a sentence means is to ask someone who knows, and that person will often not be able to explain convincingly how he or she knows. Grammar manuals and dictionaries alone are not sufficient tools to help decipher many classical texts —familiarity with the culture and with literary conventions is also essential.

How can students gain fluency in reading classical texts? In the beginning they can learn from their teachers, who learned from their teachers and from traditional commentaries. After reading a certain amount—roughly the amount contained in this volume—students will begin to "get a feel" for the language, and be able to offer their own readings with some confidence. Constant review is the single most effective strategy in learning *wényán*. Flexibility is the most valuable stance from which to approach the texts.

It is useful to remember that 1) ancient texts are often concise to the point that traditional Chinese scholars themselves needed commentaries to understand them, and 2) poetic texts are often deliberately ambiguous.

Basic Vocabulary List (Two forms)

This book assumes that the student already has an intermediate knowledge of Modern Standard Chinese (two or three years of college study), and knows how to use a Chinese-English dictionary. The last part of this Introduction contains a list of about 350 characters which are commonly used in Modern Standard Chinese and which will serve as a starting point for the lessons in this text. Students should review the Basic

Vocabulary list and make sure they are thoroughly familiar with the words there before beginning the lessons.

The Basic Vocabulary list is given in two forms—first arranged alphabetically for convenient reference, and second arranged subjectively by categories (numbers, colors, family relations, etc.), an arrangement intended to be useful for purposes of review or memorization. The first version of the list contains Chinese characters; the second does not. Filling in the characters on the second version of the list is a useful preparatory exercise.

Pronunciation and Definitions

Although linguists have reconstructed the likely pronunciation of ancient and medieval Chinese, modern readers conventionally read *wényán* texts in their own dialects. This book uses the Modern Standard Chinese pronunciation, represented by the *pīnyīn* 拼音 spelling system.

Definitions in the list are necessarily brief and incomplete, and students are encouraged to consult dictionaries for further information. Please note that though the English equivalents in the list may be nouns, adjectives, or verbs, many of the Chinese words can serve as more than one part of speech.

For example: 食   *shí* can mean "food," "to eat," or "edible"
                         Pronounced *sì*, it means "to feed."
              上   *shàng* can mean "above," "high," or "go up"

Basic Vocabulary—Alphabetical List

愛	*ài*	love		地	*dì*	earth
安	*ān*	peaceful		第	*dì*	ordinal prefix
八	*bā*	eight		弟	*dì*	younger brother
白	*bái*	white		帝	*dì*	emperor
百	*bǎi*	hundred		定	*dìng*	decide, definite
半	*bàn*	half		東	*dōng*	east
寶	*bǎo*	precious; treasure		冬	*dōng*	winter
北	*běi*	north		懂	*dǒng*	understand
本	*běn*	root, trunk		動	*dòng*	move
必	*bì*	must		獨	*dú*	alone
邊	*biān*	side, border		短	*duǎn*	short
變	*biàn*	change		多	*duō*	many
辨	*biàn*	distinguish		惡	*è*	ugly
兵	*bīng*	soldier		耳	*ěr*	ear
病	*bìng*	ill		二	*èr*	two
并	*bìng*	together		反	*fǎn*	reversed
不	*bù*	no, not		飯	*fàn*	rice, food
草	*cǎo*	grass		方	*fāng*	direction; square
常	*cháng*	constant, often		飛	*fēi*	fly
長	*cháng*	long		非	*fēi*	is not; wrong
唱	*chàng*	sing		分	*fēn*	divide
車	*chē*	cart, chariot		風	*fēng*	wind
城	*chéng*	city wall, city		父	*fù*	father
成	*chéng*	complete, finish		富	*fù*	rich
出	*chū*	go out		改	*gǎi*	change, correct
處	*chù*	place		敢	*gǎn*	dare
床	*chuáng*	bed		高	*gāo*	high
春	*chūn*	spring		告	*gào*	tell
從	*cóng*	follow; from		歌	*gē*	song
粗	*cū*	coarse		各	*gè*	each
村	*cūn*	village		狗	*gǒu*	dog
打	*dǎ*	beat, hit		古	*gǔ*	old, ancient
大	*dà*	big, large		故	*gù*	old; reason; therefore
到	*dào*	arrive at		怪	*guài*	strange
得	*dé*	get, attain		關	*guān*	close; mt. pass
等	*děng*	wait, etc.		觀	*guān*	look
低	*dī*	low		官	*guān*	official
敵	*dí*	enemy		光	*guāng*	bright

歸	*guī*	return		借	*jiè*	borrow
鬼	*guǐ*	ghost		金	*jīn*	gold; metal
貴	*guì*	valuable		今	*jīn*	today, modern
國	*guó*	kingdom		進	*jìn*	enter, advance
果	*guǒ*	fruit; result		近	*jìn*	near
過	*guò*	go over; fault		京	*jīng*	capital city
海	*hǎi*	sea		靜	*jìng*	be quiet
好	*hǎo*	good		敬	*jìng*	respect
喝	*hē*	drink		九	*jiǔ*	nine
合	*hé*	come together		酒	*jiǔ*	wine
河	*hé*	river		舊	*jiù*	old
黑	*hēi*	black		舉	*jǔ*	raise
很	*hěn*	very		居	*jū*	reside
恨	*hèn*	hate		決	*jué*	decide
紅	*hóng*	red		開	*kāi*	open
後	*hòu*	back, after		看	*kàn*	look
湖	*hú*	lake		可	*kě*	be permitted
虎	*hǔ*	tiger		客	*kè*	guest, traveller
花	*huā*	flower		空	*kōng*	empty
話	*huà*	speech, language		口	*kǒu*	mouth
畫	*huà*	painting		苦	*kǔ*	bitter; suffer
壞	*huài*	bad		來	*lái*	come
歡	*huān*	enjoy		藍	*lán*	blue
還	*huán*	return		老	*lǎo*	old
黃	*huáng*	yellow		冷	*lěng*	cold
回	*huí*	return		離	*lí*	separate from
會	*huì*	assemble; able		里	*lǐ*	Chinese mile
活	*huó*	alive		禮	*lǐ*	ceremony
火	*huǒ*	fire		裡	*lǐ*	inside
雞	*jī*	chicken		利	*lì*	benefit
幾	*jǐ*	how many, several		兩	*liǎng*	two; ounce
計	*jì*	plan		林	*lín*	forest
季	*jì*	season		流	*liú*	flow
加	*jiā*	add		六	*liù*	six
家	*jiā*	home, family		龍	*lóng*	dragon
假	*jiǎ*	false		樓	*lóu*	storied building
賤	*jiàn*	cheap		露	*lù*	dew
見	*jiàn*	see, hear		路	*lù*	road
江	*jiāng*	river		綠	*lǜ*	green
教	*jiào*	teach		亂	*luàn*	disorderly

落	*luò*	fall	千	*qiān*	thousand
馬	*mǎ*	horse	前	*qián*	front, before
買	*mǎi*	buy	淺	*qiǎn*	shallow
賣	*mài*	sell	強	*qiáng*	strong
滿	*mǎn*	full	橋	*qiáo*	bridge
毛	*máo*	feather, hair	親	*qīn*	family member
美	*měi*	beautiful	青	*qīng*	blue-green
每	*měi*	every	清	*qīng*	clear
妹	*mèi*	younger sister	輕	*qīng*	light (weight)
門	*mén*	gate	情	*qíng*	feelings
夢	*mèng*	dream	請	*qǐng*	request
面	*miàn*	face	窮	*qióng*	poor
民	*mín*	people	秋	*qiū*	autumn
明	*míng*	bright, clear	取	*qǔ*	take, select
名	*míng*	name	去	*qù*	go
末	*mò*	branch, tip	全	*quán*	completely
謀	*móu*	plot, plan	熱	*rè*	hot
母	*mǔ*	mother	人	*rén*	person
目	*mù*	eye	日	*rì*	sun, day
木	*mù*	tree	肉	*ròu*	meat, flesh
難	*nán*	difficult	如	*rú*	like, resemble
男	*nán*	male	入	*rù*	enter
南	*nán*	south	弱	*ruò*	weak
內	*nèi*	within	三	*sān*	three
能	*néng*	be able	山	*shān*	mountain
你	*nǐ*	you	善	*shàn*	good
年	*nián*	year	上	*shàng*	on, go up
念	*niàn*	think of	少	*shǎo*	few
鳥	*niǎo*	bird	少	*shào*	young
牛	*niú*	cow, ox	蛇	*shé*	snake
女	*nǚ*	female	誰	*shéi*	who
怕	*pà*	fear	身	*shēn*	body, self
胖	*pàng*	fat	深	*shēn*	deep
朋	*péng*	colleague	神	*shén*	god, spirit
平	*píng*	level, peaceful	生	*shēng*	be born, alive
破	*pò*	broken	聲	*shēng*	sound
七	*qī*	seven	聖	*shèng*	sage
騎	*qí*	ride, straddle	師	*shī*	teacher
起	*qǐ*	rise, begin	詩	*shī*	poem
氣	*qì*	breath, spirit	失	*shī*	lose

食	*shí*	food; eat
石	*shí*	stone
實	*shí*	full, real
十	*shí*	ten
時	*shí*	season, time
始	*shǐ*	begin
事	*shì*	matter, affair
室	*shì*	room, house
市	*shì*	market
試	*shì*	try, attempt
是	*shì*	this; right; is
視	*shì*	look
收	*shōu*	accept
手	*shǒu*	hand
瘦	*shòu*	thin
書	*shū*	write; book
樹	*shù*	tree
數	*shǔ*	count
數	*shù*	number
霜	*shuāng*	frost
水	*shuǐ*	water
睡	*shuì*	sleep
說	*shuō*	speak
思	*sī*	think of
死	*sǐ*	die
四	*sì*	four
松	*sōng*	pine tree
雖	*suī*	although
歲	*suì*	year; years old
他	*tā*	he, she; other
太	*tài*	too; great
天	*tiān*	heaven, sky
田	*tián*	field
聽	*tīng*	listen
通	*tōng*	go through
頭	*tóu*	head
圖	*tú*	plan, diagram
土	*tǔ*	soil, earth
外	*wài*	outside
晚	*wǎn*	late

萬	*wàn*	ten thousand
王	*wáng*	king
忘	*wàng*	forget
往	*wàng*	go toward
望	*wàng*	look toward; hope
畏	*wèi*	fear
位	*wèi*	position
文	*wén*	pattern, writing
聞	*wén*	hear, smell
問	*wèn*	ask
我	*wǒ*	I
屋	*wū*	room, house
無	*wú*	not have, not exist
五	*wǔ*	five
惡	*wù*	hate
物	*wù*	thing
西	*xī*	west
喜	*xǐ*	enjoy
細	*xì*	fine, detailed
下	*xià*	under; go down
夏	*xià*	summer
先	*xiān*	first
鄉	*xiāng*	hometown
想	*xiǎng*	think of, want
小	*xiǎo*	small
曉	*xiǎo*	dawn
笑	*xiào*	laugh, smile
寫	*xiě*	write
新	*xīn*	new
心	*xīn*	heart, mind
信	*xìn*	trust
星	*xīng*	star
兄	*xiōng*	elder brother
虛	*xū*	empty
學	*xué*	imitate, study
雪	*xuě*	snow
言	*yán*	speak; words
羊	*yáng*	sheep, goat
養	*yǎng*	raise, nourish
要	*yào*	want, must

夜	*yè*	night
一	*yī*	one
疑	*yí*	suspect
已	*yǐ*	already
以	*yǐ*	take, use
易	*yì*	easy; change
意	*yì*	idea
銀	*yín*	silver
應	*yīng*	ought; respond
影	*yǐng*	shadow
用	*yòng*	use
遊	*yóu*	travel
有	*yǒu*	have, exist
友	*yǒu*	friend
又	*yòu*	again
右	*yòu*	right (direction)
魚	*yú*	fish
雨	*yǔ*	rain
玉	*yù*	jade
欲	*yù*	want, desire
源	*yuán*	origin, source
遠	*yuǎn*	far
願	*yuàn*	be willing, want
月	*yuè*	moon; month
雲	*yún*	cloud
在	*zài*	be at, exist
再	*zài*	again
早	*zǎo*	early
長	*zhǎng*	grow
真	*zhēn*	true
正	*zhèng*	upright
政	*zhèng*	government
知	*zhī*	know
智	*zhì*	wise, clever
治	*zhì*	orderly; govern
中	*zhōng*	center
終	*zhōng*	end
鐘	*zhōng*	bell
重	*zhòng*	heavy
種	*zhòng*	plant

豬	*zhū*	pig
住	*zhù*	live at
助	*zhù*	help
子	*zǐ*	son, child
姊	*zǐ*	older sister
走	*zǒu*	run
足	*zú*	foot
昨	*zuó*	yesterday
左	*zuǒ*	left (direction)
作	*zuò*	make, do
坐	*zuò*	sit

Basic Vocabulary—By Categories

Numbers

yi	one
er	two
san	three
si	four
wu	five
liu	six
qi	seven
ba	eight
jiu	nine
shi	ten
bai	hundred
qian	thousand
wan	ten thousand
liang	two; ounce
ji	how many, several
mei	every
ge	each
ban	half
shu	number
di	ordinal prefix

Colors

hong	red
huang	yellow
hei	black
bai	white
qing	blue-green
lü	green
lan	blue

Directions

li	inside
wai	outside
zhong	center
zuo	left
you	right
nei	within
qian	front, before
hou	back, after
shang	above, on, go up
xia	under, below, go down
dong	east
xi	west
nan	south
bei	north
fang	direction; square
chu	place
bian	side, border

People

jia	home, family
ren	person
fu	father
mu	mother
zi	son, child
xiong	older brother
di	younger brother
zi	older sister
mei	younger sister
qin	family member
wo	I
ni	you
ta	he, she; other
shei	how?
ming	name
shi	teacher
peng	colleague
you	friend
wei	position
wang	king
di	emperor
guan	official
sheng	sage
min	people
bing	soldier

di	enemy	*qing*	feelings
gui	ghost	*kou*	mouth
shen	god, spirit	*shou*	hand
ke	guest, traveller	*zu*	foot
		er	ear
		mu	eye
		tou	head
		mian	face

Things in the Human World

zheng	government	*shan*	mountain
li	ceremony	*tian*	heaven, sky
guo	kingdom	*di*	earth
xiang	hometown	*ri*	sun, day
cun	village	*yue*	moon, month
shi	market	*xing*	star
cheng	city wall, city	*shui*	water
jing	capital city	*huo*	fire
shi	room, house	*qi*	breath, spirit
wu	room, house	*jiang*	river
lou	storied building	*he*	river
men	gate	*hu*	lake
lu	road	*hai*	sea
qiao	bridge	*shi*	stone
che	cart, chariot	*jin*	gold; metal
li	Chinese mile	*yin*	silver
chuang	bed	*yu*	jade
meng	dream	*tu*	earth, soil
shi	poem	*tian*	field
hua	painting	*feng*	wind
ge	song	*yu*	rain
jiu	wine	*yun*	cloud
rou	meat, flesh	*shuang*	frost
fan	rice, food	*xue*	snow
wen	pattern, writing	*lu*	dew
hua	speech	*ying*	shadow
sheng	sound	*lin*	forest
zhong	bell	*cao*	grass
wu	thing	*mu*	tree
shi	matter, affair	*hua*	flower
yuan	source		
shen	body, self		
xin	heart, mind		
yi	idea		

The "Things in the Natural World" heading appears in the second column: **Things in the Natural World**

shu	tree; to plant	*lao*	old
guo	fruit; result	*shao*	young
song	pine tree	*nan*	male
ben	root, trunk	*nü*	female
mo	branch, tip	*xin*	new
niao	bird	*jiu*	old
ma	horse	*chang*	long
niu	cow, ox	*duan*	short
yang	sheep, goat	*gao*	high
zhu	pig	*di*	low
ji	chicken	*hao*	good
gou	dog	*huai*	bad
hu	tiger	*shan*	good
she	snake	*zhi*	wise, clever
long	dragon	*mei*	beautiful
yü	fish	*e*	ugly
mao	feather, hair	*guai*	strange

Time and Seasons

ri	sun, day	*zhen*	true
yue	moon, month	*jia*	false
nian	year	*fu*	rich
sui	year, years old	*qiong*	poor
ye	night	*gui*	valuable
zuo	yesterday	*jian*	cheap
xiao	dawn	*shen*	deep
shi	time, season	*qian*	shallow
ji	season	*shi*	full
chun	spring	*xu*	empty
xia	summer	*man*	full
qiu	autumn	*kong*	empty
dong	winter	*nan*	difficult
shi	begin	*yi*	easy
zhong	end	*leng*	cold
		re	hot
		pang	fat
		shou	thin

Qualities

da	big, large	*zao*	early
xiao	small, little	*wan*	late
duo	many	*gu*	old, ancient
shao	few	*jin*	today, modern
		gu	old

yuan	far, distant	*fei*	wrong; is not
jin	close, near	*you*	have, exist
qing	light	*wu*	not have, not exist
zhong	heavy	*zai*	be at, exist
zhi	orderly (govt.)	*zhi*	know
luan	disorderly	*wang*	forget
zheng	upright	*yao*	want, must
fan	reversed	*xiang*	think, want
xian	first	*yuan*	be willing, want
qing	clear	*yu*	want
xi	fine, detailed	*gan*	dare
cu	coarse	*neng*	be able
qiang	strong	*ke*	be permitted
ruo	weak	*ying*	ought; respond
po	broken	*yong*	use
ku	bitter; suffer	*yi*	take, use
bing	ill	*jie*	borrow
du	alone	*jia*	add
ping	level, peaceful	*zuo*	make, do
an	peaceful	*kan*	look
ming	bright, clear	*shi*	look
guang	bright	*guan*	look
bao	precious	*ting*	listen

Adverbs

bu	no, not	*jian*	see, hear
tai	too, great	*da*	beat
hen	very	*lai*	come
yi	already	*qu*	go
zai	again	*wang*	go toward
you	again	*chu*	go out
bi	must	*ru*	enter
quan	completely	*deng*	wait
bing	together	*shuo*	speak
sui	although	*yan*	speak, words
chang	constant, often	*gao*	tell
ru	be like, resemble	*chang*	sing
		xie	write
		shu	write; book
		shu	count

Verbs

shi	this; right; is	*dong*	understand
		pa	fear

wei	fear	*huan*	return
jiao	teach	*gui*	return
mai	buy	*tong*	go through
mai	sell	*he*	come together
zou	run	*ai*	love
fei	fly	*wu*	hate
wen	ask	*hen*	hate
qing	request	*jing*	respect
wen	hear, smell	*xin*	trust
qi	ride, straddle	*zhu*	help
zuo	sit	*shou*	accept
sheng	be born, alive	*you*	travel
si	die, dead	*shi*	lose
huo	alive	*de*	get, attain
zhang	grow	*qu*	take, select
zhu	live at	*jing*	be quiet
ju	reside	*dong*	move
li	separate from	*fen*	divide
hui	assemble; able	*cheng*	complete, finish
kai	open	*liu*	flow
guan	close	*luo*	fall
nian	think of	*zhong*	plant
si	think of	*yang*	nourish
cong	follow; from	*jue*	decide
dao	arrive at	*ding*	decide, definite
ju	raise	*tu*	diagram, plan
wang	look toward	*ji*	plan
yi	suspect	*li*	benefit
qi	rise, begin	*guo*	go over; fault
xue	imitate, study	*gai*	change, correct
shi	try, attempt	*bian*	change
mou	plot, plan		
xiao	smile, laugh		
xi	enjoy		
huan	enjoy		
bian	distinguish		
shi	eat; food		
he	drink		
shui	sleep		
hui	return		

Lesson 1

Structural Principles

Traditional Chinese grammarians divided words into two categories: "empty" 虛 (*xū*) and "full" 實 (*shí*). "Empty" words are so-called "function words" or "particles." "Full" or "content" words name a thing, action, or quality. The dividing line between function and content words is not hard and fast; a given character may serve sometimes as an "empty" word and at other times as a "full" word. Examples of "empty" words are *yīn* 因 (because of), *yǐ* 以 (in order to), *yú* 於 (at), *bù* 不 (not), and *yǔ* 與 (and). Examples of "full" words are *wáng* 王 (king), *dì* 地 (earth), *hóng* 紅 (red), *xiǎo* 小 (small), *hǎo* 好 (good), *zǒu* 走 (run), *fēi* 飛 (fly), *qián* 前 (front), and *shàng* 上 (top, go up).

This lesson uses only "full" words.

The simplest structures in *wényán* consist of two concrete ("full") words juxtaposed. There are four basic ways in which the two words can relate to each other:

1) Modifier → Modified

好王　*hǎo wáng* = good king
紅花　*hóng huā* = red flower
山林　*shān lín* = mountain forest
東流　*dōng liú* = eastward flow; flow eastward
遠思　*yuǎn sī* = distantly think; think of from afar

2) X and Y (where X and Y are balanced terms)

天地　*tiān dì* = heaven and earth
父母　*fù mǔ* = father and mother
黑白　*hēi bái* = black and white
日夜　*rì yè* = day and night
日月　*rì yuè* = sun and moon; day and month
古今　*gǔ jīn* = ancient and modern

3) Subject → Predicate (or) Topic → Comment

我去　*wǒ qù* = I go
天黑　*tiān hēi* = the sky grows dark
鳥飛　*niǎo fēi* = the (a) bird flies or birds fly
馬死　*mǎ sǐ* = (the/a) horse(s) die(s)
花紅　*huā hóng* = (the/a) flower(s) is/are red
人大　*rén dà* = (the/a) person is large

4) Verb → Object

    騎馬   *qí mǎ* = ride the/a horse

    看花   *kàn huā* = look at flower(s)

    食肉   *shí ròu* = eat meat

    畫畫   *huà huà* = paint a painting

    開門   *kāi mén* = open the gate

    見山   *jiàn shān* = see the mountain(s)

Note that:

1. Number and tense are indefinite unless explicitly specified, or implied by context.

2. The relation between juxtaposed words is determined by the semantic content of the words themselves as well as by the context in which they occur. Often the relation between isolated pairs of words can be ambiguous, e.g.:

    月下   *yuè xià* = under the moon; the moon descends

    流水   *liú shuǐ* = flowing water; cause the water to flow

    人生   *rén shēng* = a person is born; human life

    山林   *shān lín* = mountains and forest; mountain forest

    A larger context usually suggests which reading is appropriate.

3. The four relationships presented above can be made explicit by use of particles or other structural devices. Several of these particles will be introduced in subsequent lessons.

Larger word groups follow the same four patterns illustrated above. Their component parts combine to make larger structures:

    水鳥 飛   *shuǐ niǎo fēi* = water-birds fly

    月 近人   *yuè jìn rén* = the moon draws near the person

    白頭 人   *bái tóu rén* = white-haired person

    打 落水狗 *dǎ luò shuǐ gǒu* = beat a dog who has fallen into the water

    深入 人心 *shēn rù rén xīn* = deeply enter people's hearts

Parallelism

One of the most important stylistic devices in *wényán* is the use of parallelism — two phrases with the same grammatical structure juxtaposed to each other. The simplest form is to juxtapose two two-character phrases of the types illustrated above:

    一舉兩得   *yī jǔ liǎng dé* = lit., one action two attainments; "kill two birds with one stone"

敵強我弱　　*dí qiáng wǒ ruò* = the enemy is strong and we are weak

天南地北　　*tiān nán dì běi* = lit., south of heaven and north of earth; poles apart

Notice that the two parallel phrases often contain pairs of opposites or balanced terms such as 高 and 低 , 多 and 少, 日 and 月 .

Parallel phrases are common in all kinds of classical texts, including philosophical and historical works as well as poetry, and developing the ability to recognize them will greatly increase one's skill in reading *wényán*. The last two lines in the poem at the end of this lesson are an example of parallelism in poetry.

Set Phrases or "Chengyu" 成語

Both classical and modern Chinese contain hundreds of set phrases, called *chéngyǔ*, which are usually four-character classical phrases, often consisting of two parallel terms. *Chéngyǔ* have a status similar to proverbs in other languages, and are used in both speech and writing to impart a lively or sometimes literary quality, depending on the *chéngyǔ* used. Below are several common *chéngyǔ* used in modern Chinese, derived from the structural principles introduced above.

開門見山　　*kāi mén jiàn shān*
　　　　lit., open the door and see the mountain;
　　　　means "get straight to the point," "don't beat around the bush."

騎虎難下　　*qí hǔ nán xià*
　　　　lit., (if you) ride a tiger (it is) hard to get off;
　　　　means to be involved in something that is hard to get out of.

走馬看花　　*zǒu mǎ kàn huā*
　　　　lit., look at flowers while on a running horse;
　　　　means to give something a cursory glance.

人山人海　　*rén shān rén hǎi*
　　　　lit., human mountain and human sea,
　　　　means a huge crowd of people.

少見多怪　　*shǎo jiàn duō guài*
　　　　lit., the less one sees the more one wonders
　　　　describes an ignorant person who is easy to amaze.

Exercises

1. Give the meanings for each of the following two-character phrases. Explain the structural relation between the two characters in each example, and state which pairs are ambiguous.

1.	三國	11.	男女
2.	日出	12.	前後
3.	作詩	13.	下馬
4.	我知	14.	飛鳥
5.	山高	15.	舉頭
6.	小車	16.	山水
7.	鳥飛	17.	中國
8.	多言	18.	看花
9.	四海	19.	上山
10.	床前	20.	王死

2. Give the meanings and explain the structures of the following three-character phrases, all of which come from Tang poems.

1. 春山 空
2. 地上 霜
3. 滿 天地
4. 思 故鄉
5. 白雲 飛
6. 望 明月
7. 幾萬 里
8. 天上 月

9. 秋風　生
10. 花木　深
11. 明月　光
12. 出門　看

3. Below is a well-known poem by the Tang poet *Lǐ Bái* 李白 (701-762). The poem consists of four lines of five characters each. Typically, in five-character lines the first two characters have a close syntactic relation to each other, followed by a pause or caesura, and the last three also form a syntactic unit. Note that in Chinese poetry it is not necessary to specify whether the subject is "I" or "he/she."

夜思

床前　明月光
疑是　地上霜
舉頭　望明月
低頭　思故鄉

Notes

Introduction

Lessons 2-8 introduce *wényán* particles and present authentic texts or fragments of texts from Chinese poetry, philosophy, and history. Each Lesson has a set of **Active Vocabulary** words, which the student should memorize. Additional, less common vocabulary items are annotated within the texts as they occur.

Vocabulary Notes may contain both cultural information and grammatical or structural explanations. Since most classical Chinese texts are written from a Confucian or Daoist perspective, it is impossible to understand many of them without a knowledge of these world-views, no matter how good one's grasp of the linguistic structures may be. Some relevant notes are included in these lessons, but students are strongly encouraged to read a good introductory work on early Chinese thought in order to become more familiar with Confucian and Daoist ideas and terminology. Other **Cultural Notes**, not specific to Vocabulary, briefly introduce some major literary forms.

The **Exercises** section contains phrases, sentences, or entire short works from the classics. For some of the more difficult selections, English translations are provided for reference.

Each Lesson also introduces five *chéngyǔ* derived from Classical Chinese, which are commonly used in contemporary Chinese texts.

Active Vocabulary

君	*jūn*	lord; you (polite)
君子	*jūnzǐ*	gentleman
子	*zǐ*	you (polite); Master
曰	*yuē*	to say, introducing a direct quote
小人	*xiǎorén*	petty person
道	*dào*	path; the Way; to say
命	*mìng*	command; fate
之	*zhī*	subordinating particle; him, her, it
其	*qí*	his, her, its; this, that
似	*sì*	be like, resemble
者	*zhě*	one who… ; marker for topic
而	*ér*	and, but
皆	*jiē*	all
朝	*zhāo*	morning
懷	*huái*	think about, remember fondly; embrace
霧	*wù*	mist
志	*zhì*	goal, will, aspiration

Proper Names

孔子	*Kǒng Zǐ*	Confucius, Chinese thinker (551-479 B.C.)
孟子	*Mèng Zǐ*	Mencius, Confucian thinker (372-289 B.C.)
老子	*Lǎo Zǐ*	Lao Zi (Lao Tzu), Daoist thinker, dates unknown.
李白	*Lǐ Bái*	Li Bai (Li Po), poet (701-762)
白居易	*Bái Jūyì*	Bai Juyi (Po Chü-yi), poet (772-846)
李煜	*Lǐ Yù*	Li Yu, poet (937-978)
論語	*Lúnyǔ*	*Analects* (Sayings of Confucius and his disciples)
孟子	*Mèngzǐ*	*Mencius* (Writings of Mencius; this book and the *Analects* 論語 are the two primary early Confucian texts.)

Vocabulary Notes

1. 君，子，君子，小人 *jūn, zǐ, jūnzǐ, and xiǎorén*

Jūn by itself means "lord" or "prince." It is also often used as a polite term of address to a man of high social status: "You, sir."

Zǐ means "offspring," or specifically "son(s)." Like *jūn* it is also used as a term of direct address: "you."

Zǐ is used with the surnames of some of the ancient philosophers as a title of respect:

孔子	*Kǒngzǐ*	Master Kong = Confucius
孟子	*Mèngzǐ*	Master Meng = Mencius
老子	*Lǎozǐ*	The Old Master = Lao Tzu; Lao Zi

In the Confucian *Analects* 論語, from which several of the passages in this textbook are taken, 子曰 *zǐ yuē* means, "The Master (= Confucius) said."

Confucius used the term *jūnzǐ*, or Lord's Son, to denote a person who was a Gentleman in a moral, not merely a social, sense. The term is now associated with the Confucian ideals of character and behavior. The opposite of a *jūnzǐ* is a *xiǎorén* (small/ petty person), a common, unrefined, self-serving individual.

2. 道 *dào*

Dào, literally "path" or "way," refers also to a philosophical principle in both Confucian and Daoist thought. The term has a range of meanings varying from "the supreme force that regulates the universe" to the "way" or "method" of performing a mundane task, as well as its primary meaning of "path."

Dào also means "to speak," "to say."

3. 天 *tiān*

The basic meaning of *tiān* is "sky;" a related meaning is a philosophical or religious principle similar to the Dao. In its first meaning it is contrasted with 地 *dì* "earth;" in its second meaning it is often contrasted with 人 *rén* "mankind." *Tiān* can also mean "day," as in modern Chinese.

Some common compounds with *tiān*:

天下	under heaven = the whole earth, the world
天子	Son of Heaven = the emperor
天命	Heaven's Command = the Mandate of Heaven
	(concerning who should rule on earth)

4. 萬物   *wàn wù*

Wànwù, "10,000 things," "the myriad creatures," refers to all things on earth. The term is often used in Daoist texts.

5. 有，無   *yǒu, wú*

Yǒu means "to have," "to exist," "there are. . ." *Wú* is the opposite of *yǒu*: "not to have," "not to exist," "there is no. . ."

Examples:

有名	having a name; the named
無名	not having a name; the unnamed; nameless
無聲	without a sound
有人知	there are people who know
無人知	no one knows

6. 是，非   *shì, fēi*

When *shì* and *fēi* are used as substantive or descriptive words, *shì* means "right," "correct," "true" and *fēi* means "wrong," "incorrect," "false."

As a verb or copula, *shì* can be used in its modern sense of "to be," but this use is not common in *wényán*. *Fēi* is more commonly used as a verb, and means "is/are not."

Shì is also used as a demonstrative pronoun, meaning "this."

Shìfēi as a phrase means "right and wrong," "true and false."

Examples:

如是	like this
是人	this person
在是	here
無是	without this
明辨是非	clearly distinguish right from wrong

7. 言，曰   *yán, yuē*

Yán can mean "words," "what is said," and can also mean "to say." In the latter case it usually introduces an indirect quote.

Yuē is used to introduce a direct quotation.

Examples:

聖人之言	the words of the sages (for use of 之 see #9 below)
子曰	The Master said: "..."
詩曰	[The Book of] Poetry said: "..."

8.   好   *hǎo, hào*

Note that in *wényán* the word *hào* (fourth tone) is often used as a verb, meaning "to like," "to be good at," in addition to its third-tone use as a modifier "good."

Examples:

好學	love to study
好古	love the ancient [things/ways]

9.   之   *zhī*

One of the most frequently encountered *wényán* particles is *zhī*. It has several different uses; two are introduced here, and others will appear in later lessons.

a) *Zhī* can function as a subordinating particle equivalent to 的 *de* in modern Chinese. In this pattern it connects two substantive words or phrases.

Examples:

李白之詩	Li Bai's poems
天之道	the Way of Heaven
少之時	the time when he/she was young
人之正道	the proper path for mankind

b) *Zhī* can also function as a third-person pronoun "him," "her," "it," as the object of a verb.

Examples:

用之	use it
知之	know it
笑之	laugh at him/her/it

10.   其   *qí*

Qí is often a third-person pronoun: "his," "hers," "its," "their."

Examples:

其國	his kingdom
其言	his words, what he says
正其心	rectify his heart

It can also mean "this," "that," "these," or "those."

Examples:

其後	after this
其時	at that time
其中	among them

11. 如，似   *rú, sì*

Rú and *sì* both introduce comparisons or similes.

Examples:

花如雪   flowers resemble snow
似舊時   like old times
如一夢   as in a dream
似朝雲   like the morning clouds

12. 者   *zhě*

Zhě can be used as a suffix to mean "one who does or is X."

Examples:

學者   one who studies; a scholar
老者   old one(s)
美者   beautiful one(s)
無知者   those who don't know anything

13. 而   *ér*

Ér, meaning "and" or "but," connects two verbal elements. The element before the *ér* frequently modifies or presents a condition for the main verb which follows.

少而好學   is young and likes to study/ likes to study when young
敬鬼神而遠之   Respect ghosts and spirits, but keep them at a distance.
                        (*Lunyu*)

14. (遠之 **keep them at a distance**)

Note that in the last example in 13 above, 遠 is used in a transitive sense, "to distance, to keep at a distance." Words which are normally considered intransitive or stative verbs are often used this way in *wényán*.

Examples:

貴之   consider it to be valuable
智其子   consider his son to be wise (智 *zhì*—wise)
難之   make things difficult for him

Exercises

Phrases

1. 如春夢

2. 天地之始

3. 君之子

4. 萬物之母

5. 先成者

6. 治其國

7. 霜如雪

8. 有女如雲

9. 先王之道

10. 美人如花

11. 天下之正道

Sentences

12. 天長路遠

13. 有客從外來

14. 君子愛之

15. 君之意 我已知之

16. 是非之心 人皆有之 （孟子）

17. 無人知其意

18. 王曰：善

Lines from Poems (all from Li Bai 李白)

(The space between groups of characters indicates the basic structural or syntactic division of the line.)

1. 明月　出天山

2. 長風　幾萬里

3. 不見　有人還

4. 海鳥　知天風

5. 早起　見日出

6. 五月　天上雪

7. 望望　不見君

8. 今人　不見　古時月

Poem by Bai Juyi　白居易

花非花

花非花，霧非霧，夜半來，天明去。

來如春夢　不多時，去似朝雲　無覓處。

覓　　　*mì*　　　search for, find

Poem by Li Yu　李煜

Li Yu, also known as Li Hou Zhu　李後主, was king of the Southern Tang, one of the short-lived states that succeeded the Tang dynasty. His kingdom was conquered by the Song dynasty in 974, and he was taken north into captivity, where he wrote many lyric poems including this one, poignantly recalling his earlier life of luxury.

望江南

多少恨？昨夜夢魂中，還似舊時遊上苑。

車如流水　馬如龍，花月正春風。

魂　　　*hún*　　　soul
苑　　　*yuàn*　　　garden

Edifying verse from an anecdote by Liu Xiang 劉向

少而好學，如日出之陽

壯而好學，如日中之光

老而好學，如炳燭之明

陽	*yáng*	bright
壯	*zhuàng*	robust, prime of life
炳	*bǐng*	luminous
燭	*zhú*	candle

Selections from the *Analects* 論語

1. 子曰：君子謀道而不謀食。　(15.31)

2. 子曰：不在其位，不謀其政。(8.14)

3. 子路曰：願聞子之志。

　　子曰：老者安之，朋友信之，少者懷之。 (5.25)

　　　子路　*Zǐlù*–a disciple of Confucius

4. 事君　敬其事而後其食。(15.37)

Selections from Lao Zi 老子

1. 道可道，非常道。名可名，非常名。(Ch. l)

2. 無名，天地之始。　有名，萬物之母。 (Ch. 1)

3. 知者不言，言者不知。(Ch. 56)

4. 信者不美，美者不信。(Ch. 81)

For reference—Literal (not literary) translations for poems and selections from *Analects* **and** *Lao Zi.* (Please note that there are valid alternative interpretations for virtually all these texts.)

Bai Juyi poem: A flower and yet not a flower, mist and yet not mist. [She] comes at midnight, and leaves at dawn. She comes like a spring dream, for a short time, and leaves like the morning clouds, with no place to find her.

Li Yu poem: How much suffering [can I endure]? Last night in my dream soul I seemed to return to wander in the gardens of former times. The chariots were like a stream of water, the horses like a dragon [a long curved line of horses]. The flowers and moon gave exactly a spring atmosphere.

Analects:
1. The Master said: A Gentleman concerns himself with the Way and not with his livelihood (food).
2. The Master said: When one is not in a given office, one should not concern himself with the tasks of that office.
3. Zilu said: I would like to hear your goals. The Master said: As for the old ones, let them rest. As for friends and colleagues, be trustworthy to them. As for the young ones, cherish them.
4. When serving a lord, respect your task and pay secondary attention to your food (salary).

Lao Zi:
1. The Way that can be spoken of is not the constant Way. The Names that can be named are not the constant Names.
2. The Nameless is the beginning of Heaven and Earth; the Named is the Mother of the ten thousand things.
3. Those who know do not speak; those who speak do not know.
4. Trustworthy words are not beautiful; beautiful words are not trustworthy.

Chengyu

[Explain the literal meaning, then check a dictionary to find how each expression is used.]

1. 口是心非
2. 似是而非
3. 如魚得水
4. 志同道合
5. 車水馬龍

Notes

Lesson 3

Active Vocabulary

仁	*rén*	humaneness, benevolence
義	*yì*	righteousness, duty
德	*dé*	virtue, moral power
孝	*xiào*	filial piety
陰	*yīn*	dark, nurturing principle
陽	*yáng*	light, creative principle
此	*cǐ*	this, these
也	*yě*	final particle
謂	*wèi*	say, be called
即	*jí*	be the same as
為	*wéi*	be, do, act as
猶	*yóu*	be like
指	*zhǐ*	finger, point to, refer to
所	*suǒ*	place; that which
矣	*yǐ*	final particle showing change of state
若	*ruò*	if; like
則	*zé*	then
於,于	*yú*	at, by, to, etc.
復	*fù*	again; return; repeat
未	*wèi*	not yet
亦	*yì*	also
吾	*wú*	I, my
止	*zhǐ*	stop, rest
由	*yóu*	from, by

至	*zhì*	arrive at, extreme, highest
臣	*chén*	minister; government servant; I, your servant
誠	*chéng*	sincere; sincerity
致	*zhì*	extend, give
閑	*xián*	at leisure
但	*dàn*	only
照	*zhào*	shine on

Proper Names

大學	*Dàxué*	*The Great Learning*, an early Confucian text
王維	*Wáng Wéi*	Tang poet (701-761)
宋	*Sòng*	name of an early Chinese kingdom, and a later dynasty
道德經	*Dào Dé Jīng*	*The Way and Its Power*, an early Daoist classic ascribed to Lao Zi

Vocabulary Notes

1. 仁，義　　*rén, yì*

Rén is the primary virtue taught by Confucius. It involves treating people the way human beings should be treated, with concern and love. The character is formed from the elements 二 "two" and 人 "person". Standard English translations include Benevolence, Humanity, and Humaneness.

Yì is a virtue much discussed by Mencius. Related to, but slightly different from, *rén*, it refers to the behavior appropriate to given social relations and given situations. It is usually translated as Righteousness or Duty. *Rén* and *yì* are often mentioned together as the two most fundamental Confucian virtues.

2. 德　　*dé*

Dé sometimes means Virtue or Right Conduct, but sometimes it refers to a kind of moral power that comes from following the Dao or the Way. The term is used by Daoists and Confucians alike. It is part of the title of the work ascribed to Lao Zi, the *Dào Dé Jīng* 道德經, lit., The Classic of the Way and [Its] Power.

3. 孝　　*xiào*

Xiào, or Filial Piety, is another of the traditional Confucian virtues. It means unquestioning obedience to one's parents.

4. 陰，陽　　*yīn, yáng*

The terms *yīn* and *yáng* refer to the fundamental oppositions of darkness (*yīn*) and light (*yáng*), of passivity and activity, of decline and growth. Many pairs of objects and qualities can be classified as *yīn* and *yáng* in relation to each other, e.g., moon/sun; night/day; female/male; mother/father; earth/heaven; cool/warm; moist/dry; nurturing/creative. The terms are used in both Confucianism and Daoism, and are fundamental concepts in fields as diverse as medicine, painting, and the martial arts. The ideal is to have balance of *yīn* and *yáng*, with neither in excess.

5. 大學　　The Great Learning

The main reading passage in this lesson is a well-known excerpt from a Confucian text called *The Great Learning*. This short text, ascribed to a grandson of Confucius, is one of the Four Books of Confucianism (*Analects*, *Mencius*, *Great Learning*, and *Doctrine of the Mean* 中庸) which formed the core of Chinese education from the Song dynasty to the beginning of the 20th century.

6. Structures of Identification or Definition

This lesson introduces some of the words and structures commonly used in both classical and modern commentaries and explanatory notes, including dictionary definitions. All these structures occur in ordinary texts too, when terms need to be defined or explained.

a) One structure commonly used to define words or to express equivalence is

X (者) Y (也)   X is/means Y

The *zhě* in this case marks the end of the topic to be defined or identified; the *yě* marks the end of the defining or identifying comment. One or both of the particles may be omitted.

仁者人也	*Rén* means "human, humanity."
仁者心之德	Humanity is the virtue of the heart.
之是也	*Zhī* means "this."
身我也	*Shēn* means "I," "myself."

b) Among the other particles commonly used to define or identify terms are the following:

曰	*yuē*	is called
謂	*wèi*	is called, means
即	*jí*	is the same as
為	*wéi*	is, acts as
猶	*yóu*	is like
指	*zhǐ*	indicates, refers to

Examples:

東西南北曰四方	North, south, east, and west are called the four directions.
此謂知本	This is called "knowing the origin."
不圖即不意	"Not to plan" is the same as "not to have in mind."
日入為夜	[When] the sun goes down it is Night.
貴猶重	"To value" is like "to give weight to."
君子指在上者	"*Jūnzǐ*" refers to the one on top [of the social hierarchy].

7. 也 *yě*

In addition to its use in sentences of identification or definition mentioned above, *yě* can serve as a final particle, giving force to an assertion, or simply marking the end of a phrase.

宋小國也	Song is a small kingdom.
天未欲平天下也	Heaven does not yet want to pacify the world.
小人不知天命而不畏也	Petty men do not know Heaven's Mandate, yet are not afraid.

8. 由 *yóu*

Yóu sometimes means "from" or "by."

由生至死   from birth to death
由學而至   arrived at by learning

Sometimes it means "follow," "allow."

小大由之   In matters small or large, we follow him.

9. 此 *cǐ*

Cǐ means "this" or "these."

此生   this life
念此   think of this
不如此   not like this, not as good as this
此五人   these five people
由此可見   from this one can see. . .
此時   this time, now

10. 所 *suǒ*

a) *Suǒ* can mean "a place."

居於王所   [He] dwelt at the king's place.
得其所   [He] achieved his [rightful] place.

b) *Suǒ* can also mean "that which," "the place which."

其所不知   what he/she did not know
我所欲學   what I want to study
所居之室   the room where he/she/they lived

c) Common combinations with *suǒ*:

所以   with which
之所以   the reason why
所由   from whence
所謂   what is called
無所不   no place where it is not = everywhere

11. 矣 *yǐ*

Yǐ is a final particle showing completed action or change of state. It is similar to the modern Chinese particle *le* 了.

吾計已決矣   My plan is already decided. / I have made up my mind.
吾不欲觀之矣   I don't want to see it any more.

12. 若，則　　*ruò...zé...*

Zé is much like the modern particle *jiù* 就. It introduces the result of the preceding action or situation, which may or may not be preceded by the word *ruò* [if].

若此則天下治　　If this is done, then the world will be in order.
吾今則可以見矣　Now I can see it.

13. 於，于　　*yú*

Yú is a general preposition showing the relation between two elements. It can indicate place or time ("at"), spacial relationship ("by," "with"), transactions ("to," "from"), and comparison ("than"), among other things. Note that two different characters may be used interchangeably for this word.

遊於四方　　　　travel in the four directions (all over the world)
子路問於孔子曰：Zilu asked (of) Confucius, saying:
無大于此　　　　none bigger than this
止於至善　　　　stop at the highest good

14. 復　*fù*

Fù means "again," "repeatedly."

復問　　　ask again
不復遠　　not go far away again
不復生　　not come back to life again

15. 未　*wèi*

Wèi means "not" or "not yet."

未來　　　　not yet come; the future
未成　　　　not yet completed, not finished
未必　　　　not necessarily
未至十里　　before they had gone ten *li*

16. 亦　*yì*

Yì means "also."

其父亦去　　His father also left.
生亦我所欲　Life is also something I desire.
道大天大地大人亦大　The Way is great, Heaven is great, Earth is great, and Man is also great.

17.   Double Negatives

Double negatives are common in Chinese, and are often used for emphasis.

無人不知   No one does not know. = Everyone knows.
無所不去   No place he/she/it doesn't go. = He/she/it goes everywhere.

18.   Full Words used as different parts of speech

Interesting stylistic effects can be achieved using the same word first as one part of speech and then as another. Here are two famous examples from the Confucian classics:

大學之道在明明德 …
The Way of Great Learning is to *make bright* the *bright* virtue…

君君臣臣父父子子
A *lord* should *act like a lord*, a minister like a minister, a father like a father, and a son like a son.

19.   古之…者   *gǔ zhī…zhě*

"Those of old who. . ."

古之欲明明德于天下者
Those of old who wished to make bright their bright virtue in the world…

古之善為道者
Those of old who were good at 'doing' the Dao…

20.   Punctuation

Note that traditionally Chinese texts were not printed with punctuation marks. Readers would sometimes mark pauses in their texts with a comma or dot, but the question marks, quotation marks, and other symbols used in modern editions did not come into general use until the 20th century. In many cases, scholars still dispute how certain classical texts should be punctuated.

Exercises

Definitions or explanations of words (1-6 with punctuation, 7-19 without).

1. 多，不少也。

2. 口，人所以言食也。

3. 人者，天地之德。

4. 人之陽曰男，陰曰女。

5. 好，美也，善也。

6. 父母，生我之人也。

7. 成人成年之人也

8. 大學者大人之學也

9. 老而無子曰獨

10. 春夏秋冬曰四時

11 三月而為一時也

12. 種魚即養魚

13. 日謂太陽月謂太陰

14. 十十謂之百十百謂之千

15. 天地者生之始也

16. 禮義者治之始也

17. 君子小人之反也

18. 東日所出也

19. 義謂各得其宜　〔宜　*yí*—appropriate〕

Sentences using new grammatical particles or structures

1. 魚失水則死。

2. 父不父則子不子。

3. 孟子曰：魚我所欲也 ... 生亦我所欲也。

4. 民無所居。

5. 此非我能為也。

6. 臣之於君也，下之於上也，若子之事父。

7. 天下難事，必作於易。天下大事，必作於細。〔作，起也。〕

8. 此非人之所能為也。

9. 是知二五而不知十也。

10. 秋日非無熱。

11. 道一也。在天則為天道，在人則為人道。

12. 人之所教，我亦教之。

13. 吾今則可以見矣。

14. 吾欲去而未能也。

Sentences from Confucian texts

(The numbers in parentheses refer to chapter and verse in the *Analects* 論語 .)

1. 四海之內，皆兄弟也。(12.5)

2. 子曰：過而不改，此謂過也。(15.29)

3. 子曰：學而不思則罔，思而不學則殆。

   〔 罔 *wǎng*，無所得。 殆 *dài*，不安也。〕 (2.15)

4. 知之為知之，不知為不知，是知也。(2.17)

5. 子曰：我未見好仁者，惡不仁者。 (4.6)

6. 子曰：君子成人之美，不成人之惡。小人反是。(12.15)

7. 天即人，人即天，人之始生，得之於天也。既生此人，則天又
   在人也。(From Song Neo-Confucian writer Zhū Xī 朱熹) (既 *jì*—since)

8. 夫孝，德之本也，教之所由生也。...
   夫孝，始于事親，中于事君，終于立身。(From 孝經 *Classic of Filial Piety*)
   (夫 *fú*—introductory particle; 立 *lì*—stand, erect)

Reading Passage from *The Great Learning* 大學

　　大學之道，在明明德，在親民，在止於至善。知止而後有定，定而後能靜，靜而後能安，安而後能慮，慮而後能得。物有本末，事有終始，知所先後，則近道矣。

　　古之欲明明德於天下者，先治其國。欲治其國者，先齊其家。欲齊其家者，先修其身。欲修其身者，先正其心。欲正其心者，先誠其意。欲誠其意者，先致其知。致知在格物。物格而後知至，知至而後意誠，意誠而後心正，心正而後身修，身修而後家齊，家齊而後國治，國治而後天下平。

慮	*lù*	ponder
齊	*qí*	regulate
修	*xiū*	repair, perfect, cultivate
格物	*gé wù*	investigate things

Two Poems by Wang Wei 王維

鳥鳴澗

人閑桂花落，夜靜春山空。月出驚山鳥，時鳴春澗中。

桂	*guì*	cassia
驚	*jīng*	startle
鳴	*míng*	[bird] call
澗	*jiàn*	stream, brook

鹿柴

空山不見人，但聞人語響。返景入深林，復照青苔上。

鹿柴	*Lù Zhài*	Deer Hermitage
響	*xiǎng*	sound, echo
返	*fǎn*	return
景	*yǐng*	陽光
	返景	落日之返照
苔	*tái*	moss

Chengyu

1. 由淺入深
2. 聽天由命
3. 各有所長
4. 無所不為
5. 若有所失

Notes

Active Vocabulary

然	*rán*	yes, thus; but
以	*yǐ*	take, use, with
為	*wéi*	be, do
為	*wèi*	for
與	*yǔ*	and, with; give
莫	*mò*	none, not
何	*hé*	what? how?
弗	*fú*	not + him/her/it
自	*zì*	self; from
之	*zhī*	go
乃	*nǎi*	then, only then; be
及	*jí*	arrive at, when; as well as
遂	*suì*	follow, after that, then
矛	*máo*	spear
行	*xíng*	walk; take action; do
舌	*shé*	tongue
予	*yú*	I
或	*huò*	someone; perhaps
寧	*níng*	rather
苗	*miáo*	sprouts
飲	*yǐn*	drink

Proper Names

楊子	*Yáng Zǐ*	Yáng Zhū 楊朱 , egoist philosopher, 4th cent. B.C.?
楚	*Chǔ*	early Chinese kingdom
鄭	*Zhèng*	early Chinese kingdom
杜甫	*Dù Fǔ*	Tang poet (712-770)
韓非子	*Hán Fēi Zǐ*	legalist philosopher, 3rd Cent. B.C.
左傳	*Zuǒ Zhuàn*	an early Chinese work of history

Vocabulary Notes

1. 然 *rán*

Rán means "yes" or "thus." It can serve as a kind of suffix to adjectives to form adverbs; in this case it functions like the English "-ly."

其所以然　the reason it is thus
無若宋人然　Don't be like the man of Song. (無　here means "don't")
自然　　　　"self-thus" = natural, naturally
笑然　　　　laughing(ly)

Common compounds with *rán*:
然後　　　　afterward
然而　　　　but

2. 以 *yǐ*

Yǐ can mean "take," "use," "by means of," "in order to," "as a result of."
以一知萬　　by means of one, know 10,000
以子之矛　　use your spear
食，以食與人也　　"To feed" is to take food and give it to someone.

Yǐ is often used with *wéi* to mean "take X as Y," "treat X as Y."
以白為黑　　consider white as black
子以我為不信　　You consider me untrustworthy.
天地不仁，以萬物為芻狗 (芻 *chú*—straw)
　　Heaven and Earth are not humane: they treat the myriad creatures like
　　straw dogs. (Lao Zi)

Common compounds with *yǐ*:
是以　　　　thus, therefore
所以　　　　that by which, the reason
何以　　　　why? how?

3. 為 *wéi, wèi*

Wei has two different uses, verbal and prepositional, distinguished by tone.

Wéi (second tone) means "to act as," "to serve as," "to be," "to do." This usage appeared in the section on dictionary entries in Lesson 3. More examples:
是可為也　　　　This can be done.

我所以為此者　　The reason I did this
常道無為而無不為 The constant Way does not act, but nothing is not
done. (Lao Zi)

Wèi (fourth tone) means "for the benefit of" or "because"
為人　　　　　for [other] people
為其母　　　　for his mother
為我　　　　　for myself
楊子取為我　Yang Zi was a hedonist. (Lit., Yang Zi chose 'for myself.')
誰為為之　　Who are you doing this for?

4.　　與　*yǔ*

Yǔ has several meanings; among them are:
　"and," "with"
天與地　　　heaven and earth
詩與畫　　　poetry and painting
仁與義　　　humanity and righteousness
　"give"
與之肉　　　give him meat
少取多與　　take little and give much

5.　　莫　*mò*

Mò means "none" or "not." It is often used with *bù* 不 to form a double negative:
"none does not = all do"
莫能為也　　No one can do it.
莫不知　　　Everyone knows.
莫大於此　　None is bigger than this.
天下莫不與也 Everyone in the world will give.

6.　　何　*hé*

Hé means "what?" or "how?"
何知　　　　How do you/I know?
今日何日　　What day is it today?
問女何所思　I ask the woman what she is thinking about.
何日復歸來　When shall I return again?

Some common compounds with *hé*:
何人　　　　who?

何時	when?
何以	how? In what way?
如何	how? How would that be?
為何	why? What for?
何必	why must?

7. 弗 *fú*

Fú is a contraction of *bù* 不 and *zhī* 之 : "not + him/her/it."

弗信	not trust him/her
弗問	not ask him/her
弗可以加矣	You can't add anything to it.

8. 自 *zì*

Zì can mean "oneself," "itself," "by itself."

自愛	love oneself
自利	benefit oneself
自然	self-like, natural
自強	make oneself strong

Zì can also mean "from" (time or space)

自古	from ancient times
君自故鄉來	You have come from [our] hometown.
有朋自遠方來	to have a colleague come from afar

9. 之 *zhī*

Two meanings of *zhī* were introduced in Lesson 2. Another meaning is "to go."

| 楊子之宋 | Yang Zi went to Song. |
| 問君何所之 | I ask you where you are going. |

10. 乃 *năi*

Năi sometimes means "then," "only then."

乃止	then [he/she/they] stopped
乃曰	then [he/she] said
兵乃出	Only then did/will the soldiers set forth.
又數年乃死	After several more years he died.

Năi can also mean "to be," "is none other than."

| X 視 之 , 乃 Y 也 | X looked at him, and it turned out to be Y. |

11. 及 *jí*

Jí means "arrive at," "when," "as well as."

及其老也	when he is old
不及	not as good as, not come up to the level of
自古及今	from ancient times to the present
今日已不及	We won't get to it today.

12. 遂 *suì*

Suì means "follow," "after that," "then."

遂用之	Then he used him.
王遂命曰：	Then the king ordered: …
遂飲其酒	Then he drank his wine.

Introduction to Classical Literary Forms and Works, Part I

A. Anecdotes

Several of the reading passages in this lesson are short anecdotes from works of philosophy and history, specifically, from *Mencius*, *Han Fei Zi*, and the *Zuo Zhuan*. Anecdotes are succinct and pointed stories with clear messages, usually presented in a humorous manner. They are often used by Mencius, Han Fei Zi, and the Daoist Zhuang Zi; and indeed several early texts are entirely composed of anecdotes. Like Jesus' parables or Aesop's Fables, they present important concepts in clear and easily remembered concrete narratives. Many *chéngyǔ* derive from early anecdotes.

B. Quotations from the *Analects* and *Mencius*

In the previous lesson, and again in this lesson, there are several selections from the major Confucian classics the *Analects* and *Mencius*. It is important to understand that these two works are collections of short self-contained sayings, and not extended philosophical treatises. In *Mencius* we do sometimes find discourses that extend over a page or so of text, but more often the component passages consist only of a few sentences in isolation. It is likely that these quotations from Confucius and Mencius do not represent actual utterances of the two thinkers, but rather a distillation or crystallization of their ideas. The sentences are often concise to the point of being almost incomprehensible, and many volumes of commentary have been written to explain them.

C. Tang Poems

This lesson contains poems by Du Fu, Wang Wei, and Li Bai, three of the most famous of all Chinese poets. They all lived at approximately the same time, during the 8th century, in the middle of the Tang dynasty. Two of them, Du Fu and Li Bai, were friends, and sometimes wrote poems to each other. The poem by Du Fu in this lesson is in the *juéjù* 絕句 form, which is characterized by having four lines, all of which are either five or seven characters long. This poem, like the two poems by Wang Wei in the previous lesson, is a "five-word *juéjù*" 五言絕句. *Juéjù* are considered to be a sub-genre of *shī* 詩 poetry.

The other two poems in this lesson are *gǔ shī* 古詩, or Old Poems. *Gǔ shī* may have any even number of lines, but they too characteristically have either five or seven characters in each line. Though Li Bai's poem has eight lines, typical of the *lü shī* 律詩 or Regulated Poems, he does not follow the strict rules of parallelism required of the *lü shī* in this example.

In Tang *shī*, poets typically try to capture a particular moment in a specific natural setting. They strive to match the scene (*jǐng* 景) with a particular feeling (*qíng* 情), and to balance stillness (*jìng* 靜) with motion (*dòng* 動). Often the first part of the poem describes the scene and the second part introduces a human concern.

Conciseness

A common characteristic of all the literary forms mentioned here is the conciseness of language found in each. The ability to express complex ideas or images with only a handful of characters is the genius of the classical Chinese language, and it is exploited to the full by the great Chinese writers. This extreme economy of language provides much of the aesthetic pleasure of classical Chinese literature. But the conciseness that makes the language so powerful can also make the meaning obscure. A Chinese saying acknowledges the problem, but suggests that after repeated reading, the meaning of a text will become clear by itself: 讀書百遍，其義自見。

Exercises

Definitions

1. 以，用也。

2. 及，至也。　自後而至曰及。

3. 衣，以衣衣人也。

4. 然，是也，如此也。

5. 莫，無也，不也

6. 行，往也，去也，路也。

7. 或，疑而未定。

8. 苗，草初生曰苗。（初 *chū*—first）

Sentences

1. 此者何如也？

2. 何為其然也？

3. 吾母與弟在長安。

4. 不以兵強天下。

5. 吾雖知之，弗能言也。

6. 事雖小，不為不成。

7. 以是為非。

8. 君子以行言，小人以舌言。

9. 是以不去。

10. 子何以知之？

11. 聞其言不如得其所以言。

12. 此孔子之所以不言也。

13. 雖有至道，弗學，不知其善也。

14. 聖人無常心，以百姓心為心。

15. 目之所美，心以為不義，弗敢視也。

16. 聖人不知亂之所自起，則不能治。

Sentences from Confucian texts

1. 子曰：古之學者為己，今之學者為人。 (14.25)

2. 子曰：不知命，無以為君子也。不知禮，無以立也。
    不知言，無以知人也。 (20.3)

3. 子曰：可與言而不與之言，失人也。不可與言而與之言，失言。
    知者不失人，亦不失言。 (15.7)

4. 孟子曰：三代得天下也，以仁。其失天下，以不仁。 (*Mencius* 4a.3)
    (三代 *sān dài*–the three early dynasties 夏商周 *Xià, Shāng, and Zhōu*)

5. 孟子曰：君仁莫不仁，君義莫不義。 (4b.5)

6. 孟子曰：君子之於物也，愛之而弗仁。於民也，仁之而弗親。
    親親而仁民，仁民而愛物。 (7a.45)

7. 孟子曰：不孝有三，無後為大。... (4a.26)

8. 孟子曰：仁之實，事親是也。義之實，從兄是也。... (4a.27)

9. 孟子曰：非禮之禮，非義之義，大人弗為。 (4b.6)

10. 孟子曰：楊子取為我，拔一毛而利天下，不為也。(7a.26)
    (拔 *bá*—pluck, pull out)

Four Anecdotes

1. From 孟子 2a.2

揠苗助長

宋人有閔其苗之不長而揠之者。芒芒然歸，謂其人曰：「今日病矣。
予助苗長矣。」其子趨而往視之，苗則槁矣。天下之不助苗長者寡矣。

閔	*mǐn*	worry about
揠	*yà*	pull up, tug on
芒芒然	*mángmángrán*	tired, exhausted
趨	*qū*	hurry, rush
槁	*gǎo*	dried up
寡	*guǎ*	少也

2. From 左傳

宋人獻玉

宋人或得玉，獻諸子罕，子罕弗受。獻玉者曰：「以示玉人，玉人以為寶也，故敢獻之。」子罕曰：「吾以無貪為寶，爾以玉為寶。若以與我，皆喪寶也。不若人有其寶。」

獻	*xiàn*	present to a superior
諸	*zhū*	contraction of 之於
子罕	*Zǐhǎn*	人名
示	*shì*	show
玉人	*yùrén*	"jade man," jade expert
貪	*tān*	greedy
爾	*ér*	you
喪	*sàng*	mourn; lose
不若	*búruò*	it would be better to, might as well

3. From 韓非子

矛盾

楚人有鬻盾與矛者，譽之曰：「吾盾之堅，物莫能陷也。」又譽其矛曰：「吾矛之利，於物無不陷也。」或曰：「以子之矛，攻子之盾，何如？」其人弗能應也。

鬻	*yù*	即賣
盾	*dùn*	shield
譽	*yù*	praise
堅	*jiān*	strong, sturdy
陷	*xiàn*	penetrate
利	*lì*	(here) sharp
攻	*gōng*	attack

4. From 韓非子

鄭人置履

鄭人有且置履者，先自度其足而置其坐。至之市而忘操之。已得履，乃曰：
「吾忘持度。」反歸取之。及之，市罷，遂不得履。人曰：「何不試之以足？」
曰：「寧信度，無自信也。」

且	*qiě*	about to
置	*zhì*	buy; put
履	*lǚ*	shoes
度	*duó*	measure
度	*dù*	measurement
市	*shì*	market
操	*caō*	take
持	*chí*	take
罷	*bà*	finish, end

Three Poems

1. 杜甫　　　絕句

江碧鳥逾白，山青花欲燃。今春看又過，何日是歸年？

碧	*bì*	jade green
逾	*yú*	more, very
燃	*rán*	burn

2. 王維　　　送別

下馬飲君酒，問君何所之。君言不得意，歸臥南山陲。
但去莫復問，白雲無盡時。

送別	*sòngbié*	send someone off
臥	*wò*	lie down
陲	*chuí*	edge, border
盡	*jìn*	end, cease

3. 李白　　金鄉送韋八之西京

客自長安來，還歸長安去。狂風吹我心，西挂咸陽樹。

此情不可道，此別何時遇。望望不見君，連山起煙霧。

(Title: At Jinxiang [in Shandong province] Sending off Eighth Master Wei, who is going to the Western Capital [Chang'an])

韋	*Wéi*	[surname]
狂	*kuáng*	wild, mad
吹	*chuī*	blow
挂	*guà*	hang
咸陽	*Xiányáng*	early capital of China, near Changan
別	*bié*	separate, part
遇	*yù*	encounter, meet
連	*lián*	connected, one after another
煙	*yān*	smoke, haze
霧	*wù*	mist

Chengyu

1. 一毛不拔

2. 以子之矛，攻子之盾

3. 愛莫能助

4. 飲水思源

5. 行成于思

Notes

Active Vocabulary

安	*ān*	how? where?
相	*xiāng*	each other, one to another
且	*qiě*	moreover
勿，無	*wù*	don't
足	*zú*	sufficient
固	*gù*	strong, rigid; definitely
而已	*éryǐ*	that is all
添	*tiān*	add
別	*bié*	separate, be apart
容易	*róngyì*	easy
初	*chū*	first, beginning
性	*xìng*	inborn nature
習	*xí*	practice
久	*jiǔ*	long time
勝	*shèng*	overcome, conquer
餘	*yú*	more than; excess
枝	*zhī*	branch
浮	*fú*	float
令	*lìng*	order, cause
忽	*hū*	suddenly
注	*zhù*	note, annotation
唯，惟	*wéi*	only
既	*jì*	already, since
經	*jīng*	pass through, experience; classic, scripture

Proper Names

莊子	*Zhuāng Zǐ*	Early Daoist philosopher (4th Cent. B.C.)
中庸	*Zhōng Yōng*	*Doctrine of the Mean* (The fourth of the four Confucian texts, or Four Books 四書 , along with *Analects*, *Mencius*, and *Great Learning*.)
戰國策	*Zhàn Guó Cè*	*Intrigues of the Warring States*, an early historical work.

Vocabulary Notes

1. 安 *ān*

   In addition to its common meaning of "peace, peaceful, pacify," *ān* is used in *wényán* as a question word, meaning "how?"

安天下	pacify the world
無有安國	There is no country at peace.
安心坐	sitting with a peaceful heart
安知	How do you know?
安可得	How can one get it?
子安能為之	How can you do it?

2. 相 *xiāng*

   Xiāng means "mutually" or "one toward another (but not necessarily mutually)."

相去	separated from each other
相思	thinking of each other (or) one thinking of the other
相看	looking at each other (or) one looking at the other
相似	resemble each other

3. 且 *qiě*

   Qiě means "moreover" or "also."

大且高	both large and high
得酒且歡喜	get some wine and enjoy oneself

4. 勿，無 *wù*

   Wù means "don't."

無復道	Don't talk about it again.

   己所不欲，勿施於人。〔論語〕(施 *shī*—do)
   Do not do to others what you would not want done to yourself.
   欲人勿聞，莫若勿言。
   If you don't want people to hear, it is better not to speak.

5. 足 *zú*

   Zú can mean "foot;" it can also mean "sufficient."

畫蛇添足	draw a snake and add feet = do something superfluous

不足	not enough
何足	how is it enough? how is it worth…?
不足觀	not worth looking at
知足	"know sufficiency," be satisfied with what one has
知足者富	One who is satisfied with what he has is "wealthy."

6.   固   *gù*

Gù can mean "strong" or "rigid." As a particle it means "definitely," "indeed."

固國	strengthen the state
蛇固無足	Snakes certainly do not have feet.
子固非魚也	You are definitely not a fish.

7.   而已   *éryǐ*

Éryǐ at the end of a phrase means something like "and that's all," "and that's the way it is."

學者學此而已   Scholars study this (and nothing else).

子曰：道二，仁與不仁而已。

Confucius said, "There are only two paths—the humane and the inhumane."

8.   **Repeated words**

It is common in *wényán*, especially in poetry, to repeat a word, indicating repetition of things or actions.

事事	everything
夜夜	every night
處處	every place
行行	walking and walking
冷冷	always cold, how cold!
念念	thinking and thinking

Cultural Notes

Daoist Texts—Lao Zi and Zhuang Zi 老子〔道德經〕，莊子

The second great Way of thought in China, after Confucianism, is Daoism. The two main texts of early Daoism are the *Dao De Jing*, ascribed to Lao Zi, and the *Zhuang Zi*, ascribed to Zhuang Zi and his followers. The authorship and date of composition of both texts is still under debate, but for practical purposes they can be considered late Zhou texts, approximately contemporary with *Mencius*.

Daoists share with Confucians a keen interest in following the Dao. They differ with the Confucians in their understanding of the nature of the Dao, and in their ideas of the role human beings should play in helping the Dao prevail in the world. Generally speaking, Confucians emphasize social order, rituals, virtuous behavior, and active regulation of society by worthy leaders, while Daoists emphasize non-action, letting the Way take its own course, and the rejection of human values such as wealth and status.

The *Dao De Jing* contains concise, often cryptic, comments and observations about the Way and its Power. It is valued for the way it embodies profound truths in a few short phrases. The *Zhuang Zi*, a much longer and more heterogeneous text, is especially prized for its illustrative stories and anecdotes, written in a humorous and lively style. Both texts are considered difficult, and individual passages in each are subject to widely varying interpretations.

Commentaries 注

All the major Confucian and Daoist texts have orthodox commentaries, and most of them have several sets of alternative commentaries and sub-commentaries as well. Commentaries are useful in finding the standard interpretation of unclear passages in the original texts.

The most important commentator for the Four Books of Confucianism is the Song dynasty writer Zhu Xi 朱熹. Lesson 5 includes a few short passages from *Mencius*, along with Zhu Xi's commentaries, to provide an introduction to this genre.

Exercises

Sentences

1. 小人安能知君子之意？

2. 四人相視而笑，遂相與為友。

3. 此物何足貴？

4. 別時容易，見時難。

5. 此事勿復道。

6. 是女知且美。

7. 人之初，性本善。性相近，習相遠。〔三字經〕

8. 是非不亂則天下治。

9. 子曰：父在，觀其志。父沒，觀其行。三年不改於父之道，可謂孝矣。
    〔沒 mò—die〕〔論 1.11〕

10. 故君子，名之必可言也，言之必有行也。君子於其言，無所苟而已矣。
    〔苟 gǒu—careless〕〔論 13.3〕

11. 禍莫大於不知足。〔老子〕〔禍 huò—disaster〕

12. 天與人不相勝也，是之謂真人。〔莊子〕

13. 誠者，自成也。。。是故君子誠之為貴。誠者，非自成己而已
    也，所以成物也。 成己，仁也。 成物，知也。〔中庸〕

14. 子曰：道不遠人。人之為道而遠人，不可以為道。〔中庸〕

15. 故君子以人治人，改而止。〔中庸〕

16. 子曰：道之不行也，我知之矣：知者過之，愚者不及也。〔中庸〕
    〔愚 yú—foolish〕

From the *Nineteen Old Poems* 古詩十九首　(anonymous, probably first or second century A.D.)

行行重行行，與君生別離。相去萬餘里，各在天一涯。

道路阻且長，會面安可知？胡馬依北風，越鳥巢南枝。

相去日已遠，衣帶日已緩。浮雲蔽白日，遊子不顧返。

思君令人老，歲月忽已晚。棄捐勿復道，努力加餐飯。

重	*chóng*	again
涯	*yá*	limit, horizon
阻	*zǔ*	hinder, obstruct(ed)
胡	*hú*	barbarian, northwestern non-Chinese
依	*yī*	lean on, rely on
越	*yuè*	Yue (southern kingdom)
巢	*cháo*	nest
帶	*dài*	sash, belt
緩	*huǎn*	loose; slow
蔽	*bì*	cover
顧	*gù*	look back, pay attention to
返	*fǎn*	return
棄	*qì*	abandon, reject
捐	*juān*	reject, cast away
努	*nǔ*	work hard
餐	*cān*	meal

Poem by Mèng Hàorán 孟浩然　(689-740 A.D.)　春曉

春眠不覺曉，處處聞啼鳥。夜來風雨聲，花落知多少？

眠	*mián*	sleep
覺	*jué*	aware
曉	*xiǎo*	dawn
啼	*tí*	call, chirp

Selections from *Mencius* 4B, with notes and/or commentaries 注

a) 　　孟子曰：人有不為也，而後可以有為。

　　注：有不為，不為非禮非義之事也。

b) 　　孟子曰：大人者，言不必信，行不必果，惟義所在。

　　朱注：主於義，則信、果在其中矣；主於信、果，則未必合義。

| 朱 | *zhū* | Zhū Xī 朱熹, Song dynasty philosopher and commentator. |
| 主 | *zhǔ* | lord; important; emphasize |

c) 　　孟子曰：大人者，不失其赤子之心者也。

　　朱注：大人之心，通達萬變。赤子之心，則純一無偽而已。然大人之所以為大人，正有以全其純一無偽之本然。是以擴而充之，則無所不知，無所不能，而極其大也。

赤	*chì*	red
赤子	*chìzǐ*	infant
達	*dá*	reach to
純	*chún*	pure
偽	*wěi*	false
擴	*kuò*	expand, enlarge
充	*chōng*	fill
極	*jí*	extreme, extend

Anecdote from the *Zhan Guo Ce* 戰國策

　　　　畫蛇添足

　　楚有祠者，賜其舍人卮酒。舍人相謂曰：「數人相飲之不足，一人飲之有餘。 請畫地為蛇，先成者飲酒。」 一人蛇先成，引酒且飲之。乃左手持卮，右手畫蛇曰：「吾能為之足。」未成，一人蛇先成，奪其卮。曰：「蛇固無足。 子安能為之足？」遂飲其酒。 為蛇足者，終亡其酒。

祠	*cí*	offer sacrifice
賜	*cì*	bestow, give
舍人	*shè rén*	retainers, underlings
卮	*zhī*	wine vessel

引	*yǐn*	pull toward oneself
奪	*duó*	grab
亡	*wáng*	lose

Lyric Poem 詞 by Bai Juyi 白居易
(a love poem, written as if spoken by a woman)

借問江潮與海水，何似君情與妾情？

相恨不如潮有信，相思始覺海非深。

借問	*jiè wèn*	(introductory phrase:) "May I ask...?"
潮	*cháo*	tide
妾	*qiè*	concubine [used by women as a humble way to refer to themselves]
恨	*hèn*	usually means 'hate'; here perhaps 'heartache,' 'pain of love'

From *Zhuang Zi* 莊子 — "The Joy of Fishes" 魚之樂
(This is a famous dialogue in which Zhuang Zi beats the logician Hui Zi at his own game.)

莊子與惠子遊於濠梁之上。

莊子曰：「儵魚出游從容。是魚之樂也。」

惠子曰：「子非魚，安知魚之樂？」

莊子曰：「子非我，安知我不知魚之樂？」

惠子曰：「我非子，固不知子矣。子固非魚也，子之不知魚之樂，全矣。」

莊子曰：「請循其本。子曰『女安知魚樂』云者，既已知我知之而問我。

我知之濠上也。」

惠子	*Huìzǐ*	early philosopher, frequent opponent of Zhuangzi
濠	*Háo*	name of a river
梁	*liáng*	bridge
儵	*tiáo*	a kind of fish
從容	*cóngróng*	carefree
樂	*lè*	joy
循	*xún*	follow
女	*rǔ*	you
云	*yún*	say (here, indicates end of a quotation)

Three Chapters from Lao Zi *Dao De Jing* 老子　道德經

(Note that each of these passages is a complete chapter. The prose is concise and cryptic. A common theme in the three passages is the need to reexamine ordinary ideas about wisdom, strength, wealth, and action, and to see the paradoxical nature of such concepts.)

第三十三章

知人者智，自知者明。勝人者有力，自勝者強。

知足者富，強行者有志。不失其所者久，死而不亡者壽。

章	*zhāng*	chapter
智	*zhì*	clever, knowledgeable
亡	*wáng*	destroy, perish
壽	*shòu*	long life

第四十章

反者，道之動。弱者，道之用。天下萬物生於有，有生於無。

第四十八章

為學日益，為道日損。損之又損，以至於無為。無為而無不為。

取天下常以無事，及其有事，不足以取天下。

益	*yì*	increase
損	*sǔn*	decrease
無事		即無為

[For reference—rough translations of one poem and the Lao Zi passages.]
From the *Nineteen Old Poems*:

> Walking and walking some more, parted from you, my lord.
> Separated by more than ten thousand *li*, each at opposite sides of the horizon.
> The road is difficult and long; how can I know when we will meet again?
> The barbarian horse leans against the north wind; the Yue bird nests on the southern branch.
> We grow farther apart every day; my robe and belt grow looser every day.
> Floating clouds cover the white sun; the traveller does not look back.
> Thinking of you makes me old; the years and months are suddenly late.
> Let it go! [*or* You have cast me aside!] Speak of it no more! Be sure you [*or* I] have enough to eat!

From Lao Zi *Dao De Jing*:

Ch. 33 One who knows others is clever; one who knows himself is enlightened.
One who overcomes others has force; one who overcomes himself has strength.
One who knows sufficiency is rich; one who is strong in his actions has a goal.
One who does not lose his place lasts a long time; one who dies but does not perish is long-lived.

Ch. 40 Reversal is the movement of the Dao; weakness [pliability] is the usefulness of the Dao.
The myriad creatures of the world are born from Being; Being is born from Nonbeing.

Ch. 48 To study, one accumulates day by day. To "do" the Dao, one loses day by day.
Losing and again losing, until one arrives at Non-action.
With Non-action, there is nothing that is not done.
To take the empire one should use non-[interference in] affairs.
When one starts meddling in affairs, one will not be able to take the empire.

Chengyu

1. 畫蛇添足

2. 添枝加葉

3. 不足輕重

4. 惟利是圖

5. 千里之行，始于足下

Notes

Lesson 6

Active Vocabulary

諸	*zhū*	all; it + preposition（之 + 於）
乎	*hū*	final particle indicating question or exclamation
就	*jiù*	go toward
夫	*fū*	man, husband
夫	*fú*	introductory particle
豈	*qǐ*	how can it be?
哉	*zāi*	final particle indicating question or exclamation
他，它	*tā*	other
焉	*yān*	how; in it, by it, therefore, therefrom, etc.
將	*jiāng*	lead; take; indicates future
將	*jiàng*	general in the army
化	*huà*	change, transform
使	*shǐ*	cause, let, allow; if
放	*fàng*	let go
求	*qiú*	seek
亡	*wáng*	lose, decline, die
存	*cún*	exist, live
文	*wén*	pattern; writing; culture
理	*lǐ*	structure; reason; principle
法	*fǎ*	law, method
愁	*chóu*	feel sad
斷	*duàn*	cut short, break off
絕	*jué*	cut off, end, extreme

感	*gǎn*	feelings, emotion
俗	*sú*	custom; common, ordinary
戰	*zhàn*	war, battle
依	*yī*	lean on, rely on, follow
樂	*lè*	joy
桃	*táo*	peach
盡	*jìn*	disappear, exhaust
舟	*zhōu*	boat

Proper Names

荀子	*Xún Zǐ*	Confucian thinker, 3rd cent. B.C.
陶潛	*Táo Qián*	poet (365-427 A.D.)

Vocabulary Notes

1. 諸 *zhū*

Zhū has two distinct meanings:

a) more than one, numerous

諸位	all of you (respectful)
諸子	the Masters (early philosophers)
諸事	various matters

b) a contraction of the words 之 + 於, 之 + 于, or 之 + 乎 meaning "it + in/by/at/etc."

君子求諸己　The Gentleman seeks it (namely, humanity) in himself.

止諸至足　　Stop it at the greatest sufficiency.

決諸東方則東流　If you lead it to the east, it will flow eastward.
(決 *jué*—here means to cut a channel for water)

2. 乎 *hū*

Hū also has two distinct uses:

a) a final particle indicating a question or exclamation

王信之乎	Does the king believe it?
其然乎其不然乎	Is that true or not?
其此之謂乎	This is what it means!
安有此事乎	How could this be?

b) a substitute for 於 or 于

好學近乎知	Loving to study is close to knowledge.
力行近乎仁	Acting with vigor is close to Humanity.
君子依乎中庸	The Gentleman relies on the Mean.

3. 就 *jiù*

Jiù in *wényán* means "go toward."

就之	go to it
孔子就楚	Confucius went to Chu.
無罪而就死地	Go to the execution ground even though not guilty.
	(罪 *zuì*—crime)
然後可以就大事	Then you can attend to great matters.

4. 夫 *fū, fú*

As a noun, *fū* means "man," and is used in compounds like these:

大夫　　　　gentleman
馬夫　　　　groom (man who takes care of horses)
夫子　　　　sage (孔夫子 Confucius)
夫婦　　　　husband and wife (婦 *fù*—woman)

夫 can also serve as an introductory particle, in which case it is pronounced *fú*.

夫誰與王敵　　Then who would oppose the king?
夫所謂先王之教者何也
　　So, what is what they call "the teachings of the former kings"?
且夫天地之間　物各有主
　　Now, in the world everything has a master.

5. 哉 *zāi*

Zāi is a final exclamatory or interrogative particle.

善哉　　　　　　Great! Wonderful!
何哉　　　　　　How can that be?
諸君其亦念之哉　You gentlemen should also think about this!
子安知吾志哉　　How can you know my ambition?

6. 豈 *qǐ*

Qǐ indicates a rhetorical question: "How can it be?"

豈不亦明乎　　How can that not be clear?
豈敢問青天　　How dare I ask the blue heaven?
王豈為是哉　　How could the king be doing it for this reason?
豈非計久長　　Isn't this planning for the long term?

7. 他，它 *tā*

Tā means "other," as in the following examples:

他人　　　other person
他日　　　another day
他國　　　other kingdoms
無他　　　nothing else
他家　　　other family (*or* other person)

8. 焉 *yān*

a) *Yān* sometimes means "how?"

焉得不老	How can one not grow old?
未知生，焉知死	Not knowing about life, how can we know about death?
焉能使人不知哉	How can you keep people from knowing?

b) Another common use combines a prepositional meaning ("at, to, with, by, from," etc.) and a previously mentioned or understood reference, to express meanings such as "therefore," "thereby," "from him," "to it," etc.

信不足焉，民不信焉

If [the king] is not sufficiently trustworthy, the people will not trust in him.

君子所性，雖大事不加焉

Even great actions can not add to a Gentleman's given nature.

民焉而不事其事

That's why ("therefore") the people do not carry out their duties.

9.　　將　　*jiāng, jiàng*

Jiāng indicates the future:

明日將至	will arrive tomorrow
知楚之將亡	knew that Chu was about to be destroyed
子將安之	Where are you going?

Jiàng means "general" (in the army)

| 古之善將 | the good generals of old |
| 為將之道，當先治心 | The way to be a general is first to control one's heart. |

Cultural Note

Mencius and Xun Zi on Human Nature

The exercises in this lesson contain famous passages from the two Confucian philosophers, Mencius and Xun Zi, discussing the major issue about which they disagreed, namely, the question of whether human nature is basically good 善 or basically 'evil' 惡 [or 'disgusting']. Mencius holds that human nature is basically good, but that it is corrupted through the vicissitudes of daily life, and that our task is to recover our lost heart. Xun Zi argues that human nature is fundamentally corrupt, but that we can perfect ourselves with civilizing influences such as rituals and study. (Gao Zi, a minor figure who appears in the Mencius passage, holds that human nature is neutral.) Xun Zi's view prevailed in China until about the ninth century; Mencius' view has been orthodox for the past thousand years.

Exercises

Sentences

1. 此不見于今，而將見于他日。

2. 天下事有難易乎？為之，則難者亦易矣。不為，則易者亦難矣。

   人之為學有難易乎？學之，則難者亦易矣。不學，則易者亦難矣。

3. 夫水行莫如舟，陸行莫如車。（陸 *lù*—dry land）

4. 戰之道，未戰養其財，將戰養其力，既戰養其氣，既勝養其心。
   〔財 *cái*—materials〕

5. 人性之善也，猶水之就下也。

6. 人性非金石，焉得久不老？

7. 歧路之中又有歧焉，吾不知所之，所以反也。
   〔歧 *qí*—fork in the road〕

From the Confucian Classics

1. 子曰：三人行，必有我師焉。　擇其善者而從之，其不善者而改之。
   〔論 7.21〕〔擇 *zé*—select〕

2. 子曰：學而時習之，不亦說乎！有朋自遠方來，不亦樂乎！

   人不知而不慍，不亦君子乎！〔論 1.1〕

   〔說 *yuè*—pleasant; 慍 *yùn*—complain〕

3. 孔子曰：君子有三畏。畏天命，畏大人，畏聖人之言。〔論 16.8〕

4. 君子如欲化民之俗，其必由學乎！〔禮記〕

5. 君子有不戰，戰必勝矣。〔孟 2b.1〕

6. 君子有三樂，而王天下不與存焉。〔孟 7a.21〕

7. 君子之道，… 雖聖人亦有所不知矣。〔中庸 12〕

Four Tang Poems

1. 王之渙　**Wang Zhihuan (8th Cent.)**　登鸛雀樓

白日依山盡，黃河入海流，欲窮千里目，更上一層樓。

登	*dēng*	ascend, climb
鸛雀	*guànquè*	stork, crane
窮	*qióng*	exhaust
目	*mù*	eye; view
層	*céng*	story (of a building)

2. 王維　**Wang Wei**　紅牡丹

綠艷閑且靜，紅衣淺復深，花心愁欲斷，春色豈知心？

| 牡丹 | *mǔdān* | peony |
| 艷 | *yàn* | beautiful, charming |

3. 崔護　**Cuī Hù (8th Cent.)**　題都城南莊

去年今日此門中，人面桃花相映紅。

人面不知何處去，桃花依舊笑春風。

題	*tí*	on the topic of
都城	*dū chéng*	the capital city , Changan
南莊	*nán zhuāng*	(place name)
映	*yìng*	reflect

4. 李白　**Li Bai**　觀放白鷹

八月邊風高，胡鷹白錦毛。孤飛一片雪，百里見秋毫。

鷹	*yīng*	falcon
胡	*hú*	Mongolian, Tartar
錦	*jǐn*	brocade, elegant
孤	*gū*	alone
片	*piàn*	(measure word) a strip, slice, flake
毫	*háo*	downy feathers

Mencius on Human Nature and on Recovering the Lost Heart

〔孟子 6a.2〕

人性善

告子曰：「性，猶湍水也：決諸東方則東流，決諸西方則西流。人性之無分於善不善也，猶水之無分於東西也。」

孟子曰：「水信無分於東西，無分於上下乎？人性之善也，猶水之就下也。　人無有不善，水無有不下。　今夫水，搏而躍之，可使過顙。激而行之，可使在山。是豈水之性哉。其勢則然也。人之可使為不善，其性亦猶是也。」

告子	*Gào Zǐ*	人名
湍	*tuān*	rapidly flowing
決	*jué*	lead water by opening a hole in a dike
信	*xìn*	固也
搏	*bó*	打也
躍	*yuè*	jump, leap
顙	*sǎng*	forehead
激	*jī*	force, urge, stimulate
勢	*shì*	power

〔孟子 6a.11〕

求放心

孟子曰：「仁，人心也。義，人路也。　舍其路而弗由，放其心而不知求，哀哉！人有雞犬放，則知求之。　有放心，而不知求。　學問之道無他，求其放心而已矣。」

舍	*shě*	set aside, let go
由	*yóu*	follow
哀	*āi*	alas!
犬	*quǎn*	dog

Xun Zi on Human Nature 荀子：性惡篇

　　人之性惡，其善者偽也。　今人之性，生而有好利焉，順是，
故爭奪生而辭讓亡焉。　生而有疾惡焉，順是，故殘賊生而忠信亡焉。
生而有耳目之欲，有好聲色焉，順是，故淫亂生而禮義文理亡焉。
然則從人之性，順人之情，必出於爭奪，合於犯文亂理而歸於暴。
故必將有師法之化，禮義之道，然後出於辭讓，合於文理而歸於治。
用此觀之，然則人之性惡明矣，其善者偽也。

篇	*piān*	chapter, section
偽	*wěi*	artificial
順	*shùn*	follow
爭	*zhēng*	strive, compete
奪	*duó*	grab
辭	*cí*	decline (a position or a favor)
讓	*ràng*	defer to someone else
疾惡	*jíwù*	jealousy and hatred
殘	*cán*	cruelty
賊	*zéi*	thief, theft
忠	*zhōng*	loyalty
色	*sè*	beauty, sex
淫	*yín*	lust, lewdness
犯	*fàn*	transgress
暴	*bào*	violence

Two Poems

鮑照　Bao Zhao (5th Cent.)　行路難

瀉水置平地，各自東西南北流。

人生亦有命，安能行嘆復坐愁。

酌酒以自寬，舉杯斷絕歌路難。

心非木石豈無感，吞聲躑躅不敢言。

瀉	*xiè*	drain, pour out
置	*zhì*	set up, place
嘆	*tàn*	sigh
酌	*zhuó*	pour
寬	*kuān*	wide, extend, relax
吞	*tūn*	swallow
躑躅	*zhízhú*	waver, be irresolute

薛濤　Xuē Tāo (女) (768-831)　柳絮

二月楊花輕復微，春風搖蕩惹人衣。

他家本是無情物，一任南風又北風。

柳絮	*liǔ xù*	willow catkins
楊	*yáng*	willow
搖蕩	*yáodàng*	waver, float
惹	*rě*	provoke, raise
任	*rèn*	allow

Poem by Tao Qian　陶潛　　歸園田居

種豆南山下，草盛豆苗稀。晨興理荒穢，帶月荷鋤歸。

道狹草木長，夕露沾我衣。衣沾不足惜，但使願無違。

豆	*dòu*	beans
盛	*shèng*	多
稀	*xī*	少
晨	*chén*	清早
興	*xīng*	起
理	*lǐ*	put in order
荒	*huāng*	wilderness, barren land
穢	*huì*	田中雜草
帶	*dài*	carry, take along
荷	*hè*	carry
鋤	*chú*	hoe
狹	*xiá*	narrow
夕	*xī*	日落時
沾	*zhān*	moisten
惜	*xī*	regret
違	*wéi*	go against
	願無違：不要違背了初願	

Tao Qian—Biographical Note

陶潛，字淵明。早年曾做過幾次小官，四十一歲任彭澤縣令，僅

八十餘日即棄官歸隱田園，直到老死。

字	*zì*	alternate name, courtesy name
淵明	*Yuānmíng* (陶潛之字)	
曾	*céng*	[indicates past event]
任	*rèn*	hold office
彭澤	*Péngzé*	地名
縣令	*xiànlìng*	官名
僅	*jǐn*	only
棄	*qì*	abandon
隱	*yǐn*	hide, seclude
直	*zhí*	straight

Two Anecdotes

1) 刻舟求劍 **from** 呂氏春秋 *Lü Shi Chunqiu* 〔漢代書名〕

　　楚人有涉江者，其劍自舟中墮于水。遽契其舟，曰：「是吾劍之所從墮。」從其所契者入水求之。舟已行矣，而劍不行。求劍若此，不亦惑乎？

刻	*kè*	carve
涉	*shè*	ford
劍	*jiàn*	sword
墮	*duò*	fall in
遽	*jù*	immediately
契	*qì*	cut a notch
惑	*huò*	doubt, foolish

2) 狐假虎威 **from** 戰國策

　　虎求百獸而食之，得狐，狐曰：「子無敢食我也。天帝使我長百獸，今子食我，是逆天帝命也。子以我為不信，吾為子先行，子隨我後，觀百獸之見我而敢不走乎？」虎以為然，故遂與之行。獸見之皆走，虎不知獸畏己而走也，以為畏狐也。

狐	*hú*	fox
假	*jiǎ*	false, pretend, borrow
威	*wēi*	might, awe
獸	*shòu*	wild animal
天帝	*tiāndì*	God
逆	*nì*	go against
隨	*suí*	follow

[For Reference—Rough translations of the passages from Mencius and Xun Zi]

Mencius

1) On Human Nature

Gao Zi said, "Human nature is like flowing water: if you lead it eastward it flows to the east; if you lead it westward if flows to the west. The way that human nature can not be categorized as [intrinsically] good or not good, is just like the way that water can not be categorized as [intrinsically] flowing eastward or westward."

Mencius said, "It is true that water may flow either east or west, but does it not distinguish between flowing upward or downward? The goodness of human nature is like the tendency of water to flow downward. There are no people who are not good, just as there is no water that does not flow downward. Now if you slap at water and splash it, you can make it go higher than your head, and if you force it along, you can make it go up a mountain. But how is this the nature of water? It does this because you force it to. The way you can make people do things that are not good is just like this."

2) On Recovering the Lost Heart

Mencius said, "Humanity is the human heart. Righteousness is the human path. If you cast aside the path and do not follow it, if you let go of your heart and do not seek it, how sad it is! If someone loses a chicken or a dog, he knows enough to go in search of it; but there are those who on losing their heart do not know enough to seek it out. The Way of Learning is nothing else but to seek out one's lost heart!"

Xun Zi

Human nature is ugly; anything good in it is artificial. Now human nature is such that from birth we love advantage (or profit). Following this [tendency] gives rise to strife and competition, and causes an end to deference and humility. From birth we are jealous and hateful. If we let these qualities go unchecked, thieves and robbers will abound and loyalty and trustworthiness decline. From birth we have the desires of ear and eye, the love of sounds and beauty. If we follow these desires, lust and disorder will arise, and decorum, righteousness, civility and reason will perish.

Thus if we follow human nature and go along with human feelings, starting from strife, we will inevitably go against civility, throw reason into confusion, and return to violence. Therefore we must make use of the transforming power of teachers and laws, and the Way of decorum and righteousness, and then starting from deference and humility we will join with civility and reason, and return to order. Looking at it this way, it is clear that human nature is ugly, and that anything good in it is artificial.

Chengyu

1. 更上一層樓
2. 刻舟求劍
3. 狐假虎威
4. 不入虎穴，焉得虎子　〔穴 *xué*—cave, lair〕
5. 豈有此理

Notes

Lesson 7

Active Vocabulary

昔	*xī*	formerly
凡	*fán*	all
彼	*bǐ*	that
當	*dāng*	suitable, ought; now, at the time
對	*duì*	face toward, reply
卻	*què*	however
否	*fǒu*	or not
尚	*shàng*	still
方	*fāng*	when, then
鄰	*lín*	neighbor
嚴	*yán*	strict, serious
器	*qì*	utensil, vessel
群	*qún*	flock, group, crowd
篇	*piān*	section of a book
講	*jiǎng*	talk, discuss
危	*wēi*	danger
寒	*hán*	cold
暑	*shǔ*	hot
智	*zhì*	wisdom, wise
勇	*yǒng*	brave
敗	*bài*	defeat; be defeated
主	*zhǔ*	lord, master; important; be in charge
賢	*xián*	worthy
直	*zhí*	straight, direct

住	*zhù*	stand, stop
塵	*chén*	dust
香	*xiāng*	fragrant
淚	*lèi*	tears
恐	*kǒng*	fear
殘	*cán*	leftover, injured
詞	*cí*	words; lyric poetry

Proper Names

孟母	*Mèng Mǔ*	Mencius' Mother (who moved three times to find a good environment in which her son could grow up)
四書	*Sì Shū*	*The Four Books* (Basic Confucian texts) 大學，中庸，論語，孟子
齊	*Qí*	Early Chinese kingdom
孫子	*Sūn Zǐ*	early military strategist
李清照〔女〕	*Lǐ Qīngzhào*	Song dynasty poet (1084?-1151?)

Vocabulary Notes

1. 昔 *xī*

Xī means "formerly," "in the past."

昔者	in the past
昔日	in former days
昔年	in former years

2. 凡 *fán*

Fán means "all," "in all cases."

凡事	all matters
凡禮之禮主於敬	All the forms of ritual are ruled by respect.
凡人莫不好言其所善	Everyone likes to talk about what he thinks is good.

3. 彼 *bǐ*

Bǐ means "that." It is often contrasted with 此 or 是 "this." Referring to a person it means "he/she/they."

彼出於是，是亦因彼。	That emerges from This, and This is a result of That.
若彼知之我計敗矣。	If he finds out about it, my plan will fail.
彼與彼年相若也。	They are about the same age as each other.

4. 臣 *chén*

Chén, meaning "government minister," was introduced in Lesson 3. It is typically contrasted with 君 "lord." Sometimes *chén* is also used by a subordinate to refer humbly to himself, "I, your servant," just as *jūn* sometimes means "you, sir."

君使臣，臣事君，如之何
    How should a lord utilize his minister, and a minister serve his lord?

臣聞求木之長者必固其本
    I have heard that someone who seeks to make a tree grow tall must first secure its roots.

5. 當 *dāng*

Dāng can mean "ought," or "correct," or "at [a particular time]."

當是時	at this time; at that time
當時之王	the kings of that time
每年當有數千萬	There ought to be several hundred thousand each year.

君子之事君也，務引其君以當道

The way for a Gentleman to serve his lord is to lead him in the right way. (務 *wù*—duty; 引 *yǐn*—lead, draw)

此愁當告誰　　　　Whom should I tell this sorrow to?

6.　對　*duì*

Duì means "to face [someone or something]." By extension it means "reply."

對飲	drink together
對敵	face an enemy, fight
孟子對曰：	Mencius replied:
對面不相見	The two sides did not see each other.

7.　卻　*què*

Què means "however."

子得半日閑，我卻忙了三日

You got half a day's leisure, but I have been working for three days.

此卻非古人之道矣

But this is not the way of the ancients.

8.　否　*fǒu*

Fǒu means "or not." It often appears in one of the following combinations:

是否	Is it or isn't it?
知否	Do you know or not?
能否	Can you or not?
可否	Is it possible or not?

9.　尚　*shàng*

Shàng means "still."

尚未能知	still can't know
尚亦有利哉	It is still beneficial.

吾固願見，今吾尚病

I certainly want to see [the king], but today I am still ill.

10.　方　*fāng*

As a particle, *fāng* means "then," "only then."

方知	then he knew
方可回矣	Only then could he return.

Introduction to Classical Literary Forms and Works, Part II

A. Treatises: Sun Zi's *Art of War*

Two kinds of prose introduced so far are anecdotes and selections from the collected sayings of early philosophers. Another kind of prose work is the treatise or essay, in which an author sets out to discuss a particular issue at some length in an organized way. One of the earliest such works in Chinese is Sun Zi's *Art of War* 孫子兵法 , from which we have a selection in this lesson. The *Art of War* has remained popular in China for over two millenia, and is now often read in business schools in the US and Asia because of the insights it offers into the strategies of attaining one's goals with the least injury to oneself.

B. Lyric poetry (*Cí* 詞)

Most of the poems in the previous lessons of this textbook have been *shī* 詩. The golden age of the *shī* was the Tang dynasty, about the seventh through the ninth centuries A.D. After that, though *shī* continue to be written, a new form called *cí* 詞 grew and flourished beside it. *Cí* means "words," and *cí* were originally lyrics ("words") to songs sung in places of entertainment. The number and length of lines of *cí* varied according to the length and rhythm of the melodies to which they were sung. As a result, there are hundreds of forms of *cí*, corresponding to the metric requirements of the various tunes. The titles of these lyric poems are often simply the titles of the original tunes, and may have no connection at all with the content of the words in the given poem. In contrast to *shī*, which often describe serious subjects in an edifying tone, *cí* frequently describe the poet's emotions; many *cí* are love poems. The poems by Li Qingzhao in this lesson are *cí*, as are the poems by Bai Juyi and Li Yu in Lesson 2.

C. Regulated Verse (*Lǜ shī* 律詩)

The last poem in this lesson, by Li Shangyin, is an eight-line *shī* which follows strict rules of tonal matching and grammatical parallelism. This kind of *shī*, which may have lines of five characters or seven characters, is known as Regulated Verse, or *Lǜ shī*. Li Shangyin's poem is a 七言律詩.

D. Children's Primers: *San Zi Jing* 三字經

A number of simple books for children became standard works which virtually all beginning students in traditional schools over the past millenium had to memorize. The three most important children's primers are:

l) The *Sān Zì Jīng* 三字經 or *Three Character Classic*, so called because each of its lines is composed of three characters. This work contains fundamental moral teachings as well as general facts of history, geography, the natural world, and so forth. Selections appear in this lesson.

2) The *Qiān Zì Wén* 千字文 or *Thousand Character Text*, a work of a thousand characters, none of which is repeated, which serves as a vocabulary builder for young students.

3) The *Bǎi Jiā Xìng* 百家姓 or *Hundred Names*, which is nothing more than a list of common surnames.

Exercises

Selections from the *Three Character Classic* 三字經

人之初，性本善。性相近，習相遠。

苟不教，性乃遷。教之道，貴以專。

昔孟母，擇鄰處。子不學，斷機杼。

養不教，父之過。教不嚴，師之惰。

子不學，非所宜。幼不學，老何為？

玉不琢，不成器。人不學，不知義。

為人子，方少時，親師友，習禮儀。

為學者，必有初。小學終，至四書。

論語者，二十篇。群弟子，記善言。

孟子者，七篇止。講道德，説仁義。

苟	*gǒu*	if
遷	*qiān*	move, change
擇	*zé*	select
機	*jī*	loom
杼	*zhù*	shuttle for weaving
惰	*duò*	lazy, remiss
宜	*yí*	suitable
幼	*yòu*	young
琢	*zhuó*	grind, polish
儀	*yí*	ceremony
弟子	*dìzǐ*	disciples
記	*jì*	record

From Sun Zi's *Art of War* 孫子兵法

a)　　孫子曰：兵者，國之大事。死生之地，存亡之道，不可不查也。
故經之以五事，校之以計，而索其情。一曰道，二曰天，三曰地，四
曰將，五曰法。

　　　道者，令民與上同意，可與之死，可與之生，而不畏危也。天者，
陰陽，寒暑，時制也。地者，遠近，險易，廣狹，死生也。將者，智，
信，仁，勇，嚴也。法者，曲制，官道，主用也。凡此五者，將莫不聞，
知之者勝，不知者不勝。

b)　　故曰：知彼知己，百戰不殆。不知彼而知己，一勝一負。不知彼，
不知己，每戰必敗。

Biographical Note:

　　　孫子，名武，春秋齊人也。善用兵。有孫子兵法十三篇。

查	*chá*	investigate
經	*jīng*	理也
校	*jiào*	比較也
索	*suǒ*	求也
情	*qíng*	事實也
制	*zhì*	control, limit
險	*xiǎn*	dangerous
狹	*xiá*	narrow
曲制	*qūzhì*	organization
殆	*dài*	perilous
負	*fù*	give in, submit
武	*wǔ*	military; (Sun Zi's given name)

Zhuang Zi's Butterfly Dream 莊子　　蝴蝶夢

昔者莊周夢為蝴蝶，栩栩然蝴蝶也。自喻適志與，不知周也。俄然覺，
則蘧蘧然周也。不知周之夢為蝴蝶與，蝴蝶之夢為周與。周與蝴蝶，
則必有分矣。此之謂物化。

蝴蝶	*húdié*	butterfly
周	*Zhōu*	莊子名周
栩栩然	*xǔxǔrán*	fluttering
喻	*yù*	understand
適	*shì*	reach, suitable
與	*yú*	final particle (interrogative or exclamatory)
俄然	*érán*	suddenly
覺	*jué*	wake up
蘧蘧然	*qúqúrán*	definitely

Poem by Hè Zhīzhāng 賀知章　(659-744)

回鄉偶書

少小離家老大回，鄉音無改鬢毛衰。

兒童相見不相識，笑問客從何處來。

偶	*ǒu*	by chance
音	*yīn*	sound, accent
鬢	*bìn*	hair on the temples
衰	*shuāi*	fade, decline
兒童	*értóng*	young boy

Yanzi Serves as Ambassador to Chu 晏子使楚，from 晏子春秋

晏子使楚，以晏子短，楚人為小門於大門側，而延晏子。晏子不入，曰：
「使狗國者，從狗門入。今臣使楚，不當從此門入。」儐者更道從大門入，
見楚王。王曰：「齊無人耶？」晏子對曰：「臨淄三百閭，張袂成陰，
揮汗成雨，比肩繼踵而在，何謂無人？」王曰：「然則子何為使乎？」
晏子對曰：「齊命使各有所主，其賢者使賢王，不肖者使不肖王。
嬰最不肖，故直使楚矣。」

晏子	*Yànzǐ*	人名，齊國大官
使	*shǐ*	serve as ambassador; ambassador
側	*cè*	邊也
延	*yán*	請也
儐	*bìn*	lead a guest
更	*gèng*	改也
耶	*yē*	虛字：乎也
臨淄	*Línzī*	既齊國都城
閭	*lú*	二十五家為一閭
張袂	*zhāng mèi*	extend sleeves
揮汗	*huī hàn*	brush off sweat
比肩	*bǐ jiān*	stand shoulder to shoulder
繼踵	*jì zhǒng*	follow close on one's heels
不肖	*bú xiào*	unworthy
嬰	*Yīng*	晏子名嬰

Two Lyric Poems 詞 **by Li Qingzhao** 李清照
(Li Qingzhao, China's most famous woman poet, is known for her exquisite sensibility.
The first poem here reflects her awareness of changes in the natural world; the second
expresses sorrow at her husband's death.)

a)　　晚春　**To the tune**　如夢令

昨夜雨疏風驟，濃睡不消殘酒。試問捲簾人，卻道海棠依舊。

知否，知否？　應是綠肥紅瘦。

疏	*shū*	sparse, far apart
驟	*zòu*	sudden
濃	*nóng*	thick, muddy
消	*xiāo*	dissolve, melt
捲	*juǎn*	roll up
簾	*lián*	blind, curtain
海棠	*hǎitáng*	crabapple, a tree with pink or red flowers
肥	*féi*	fat, plump

b)　　無題　**To the tune**　武陵春

風住塵香花已盡，日晚倦梳頭。物是人非事事休，欲語淚先流。

聞説雙溪春尚好，也擬汎輕舟。只恐雙溪蚱艋舟，載不動許多愁。

無題	*wútí*	untitled
武陵	*Wǔlíng*	地名
倦	*juàn*	tired
梳	*shū*	comb
休	*xiū*	rest, cease
雙溪	*Shuāngxī*	Double Stream 〔地名〕
擬	*nǐ*	plan
汎	*fàn*	float, sail
蚱艋	*zhámǐng*	type of small boat
載	*zài*	carry
許多	*xǔduō*	much

Poem by Zhang Ji 張繼 (768-830)　　楓橋夜泊

月落烏啼霜滿天，江楓漁火對愁眠。

姑蘇城外寒山寺，夜半鐘聲到客船。

楓	*fēng*	maple
橋	*qiáo*	bridge
泊	*bó*	moor a boat
烏	*wū*	crow, raven
啼	*tí*	bird call
漁	*yú*	to fish
眠	*mián*	sleep
姑蘇	*Gū Sū*	Suzhou (city)
寒山寺	*Hán Shān Sì*	Cold Mountain Temple
船	*chuán*	boat

Poem by Li Shangyin 李商隱 (813?-858)　　無題

相見時難別亦難，東風無力百花殘。

春蠶到死絲方盡，蠟炬成灰淚始乾。

曉鏡但愁雲鬢改，夜吟應覺月光寒。

蓬萊此去無多路，青鳥殷勤為探看。

蠶	*cán*	silkworm
絲	*sī*	silk
蠟炬	*làjù*	candle
灰	*huī*	ashes
乾	*gān*	dry
曉	*xiǎo*	dawn
鏡	*jìng*	mirror
鬢	*bìn*	hair at the temples
吟	*yín*	hum, intone
蓬萊	*Pénglái*	Island of Immortals
青鳥	*qīngniǎo*	bluebird, messenger of the immortals
殷勤	*yīnqín*	diligently
探	*tàn*	seek

[For reference—Rough translations of some passages from this lesson.]

From *San Zi Jing*

In the beginning, human nature is fundamentally good. By nature we are similar; in practice we grow apart.

If you do not teach, that nature will change. The Way of teaching is to emphasize single-mindedness.

Formerly, Mencius' mother chose her neighbors [to provide the best influences for her son]. When her son did not study, she broke her loom and shuttle [in anger at his disobedience]. [The traditional story is that she used a knife to slash the cloth she was weaving.]

To bring up [a child] and not teach him is a father's transgression. To teach and not be strict is a teacher's laziness.

From *Sun Zi's Art of War*

a) Sun Zi said, "Military affairs are an important matter for the state. One can not fail to investigate the grounds of life and death, and the ways of survival or decline.

Therefore evaluate [a given situation] in terms of the five matters [listed below], and compare them with strategies, to seek their essential conditions. [The five matters are] First: the Dao. Second: Heaven. Third: Earth. Fourth: Generals. Fifth: Methods.

The 'Dao' is what makes the people agree with their superiors, so that they are willing to die with them and live with them, and not fear danger. 'Heaven' refers to yin and yang, temperature, and the seasons. 'Earth' means distance, dangerous or easy terrain, broad or narrow roads, and whether one will live or die. 'Generals' has to do with the leaders' wisdom, trustworthiness, benevolence, courage, and strictness. 'Methods' refers to organization, use of personnel, and use of material. Generals have heard of all these five matters. Those who understand them win, and those who do not understand them do not win."

b) Therefore I say, "If you know the other and know yourself, in a hundred battles there will be no danger. If you do not know the other but know yourself, you will sometimes win and sometimes lose. If you do not know the other and do not know yourself, you will lose every battle."

Poem by Li Shangyin

Seeing one another is difficult, and parting is also difficult.
The east wind has no force, and the hundred flowers are fading.
Spring silkworms only finish spinning their silk at death,
and the candle only dries its tears when it is burnt out.
At the morning mirror I only regret my cloudlike hair is changing (turning white at the temples).
As I hum (chant poems) at night I should feel the coldness of the moonlight.
There are not many roads from here to Penglai, [the Island of the Immortals—i.e., where you live]
[I beg] the bluebird [messenger] to diligently seek you out on my behalf.

Chengyu

1. 玉不琢，不成器

2. 知彼知己，百戰不殆

3. 比肩繼踵

4. 彼一時，此一時

5. 仁者見仁，智者見智

Notes

Lesson 8

Active Vocabulary

嘗	*cháng*	taste; indicates action in the past
故	*gù*	therefore
氏	*shì*	clan, surname, Mr./Ms.
連	*lián*	connect, connected, one after another
婦	*fù*	woman
雙	*shuāng*	pair
珠	*zhū*	bead, pearl
宜	*yí*	suitable
材	*cái*	timber, material; ability
才	*cái*	talent
良	*liáng*	good
良心	*liángxīn*	conscience
等	*děng*	compare, equal
抱	*bào*	embrace, hold close to chest
妻	*qī*	wife
紙	*zhǐ*	paper
須	*xū*	need
更	*gèng*	change; even more, once more
藥	*yào*	medicine
微	*wēi*	small, slight
休	*xiū*	cease, rest
逢	*féng*	meet, encounter
鳴	*míng*	call of a bird or other animal

垂	*chuí*	hang down
沙	*shā*	sand
攻	*gōng*	attack

Proper Name

| 韓愈 | *Hán Yù* | Tang dynasty writer (768-824) |

Vocabulary Notes

1.　嘗　*cháng*

Cháng as a verb means "taste." As a particle it indicates that an event has taken place in the past.

我不敢嘗	I don't dare taste it.
嘗聽	I have heard that…
未嘗有	It has never happened.
何嘗	When has it ever…? (Answer: Never.)

上嘗欲教之吳、孫兵法
　　His highness had wanted to teach him Wu and Sun's military methods.

告子未嘗知義，以其外之也
　　Gao Zi never understood *yì*, because he treated it as something external.

2.　故　*gù*

Gù sometimes means "old," "former times":

故事	past events
故人	old (long-time) acquaintance
如故	as in the past

Sometimes it means "therefore," or "reason."

故曰：	that's why I/they say…
何故	why?
是故	for this reason
無它故	There is no other reason.
使人問其故	Have someone ask the reason for it.
故至誠如神	Therefore (one who has) ultimate sincerity is like a god.

3.　氏　*shì*

Shì means "clan." It is used following a surname to identify the family of origin of either a man or a woman. Thus, when referring to a woman, it indicates her maiden name.

王氏	Mr. Wang; someone from the Wang family
王李氏	Mrs. Wang, *née* Li.
秦氏有好女	The Qin family has a fine daughter.

4. 連 *lián*

Lián means "connect[ed]," "successive."

連日　　　　day after day
連年　　　　year after year
連山　　　　rows and rows of mountains
遂命將二十只船用索相連　　〔索 *suŏ*—rope 〕
　　Then he ordered them to tie twenty boats together with a long rope.

Mencius—Ox Mountain　孟子　(6a.8)　牛山

　　孟子曰：「牛山之木嘗美矣，以其郊於大國也，斧斤伐之，可以為美乎？是其日夜之所息，雨露之所潤，非無萌櫱之生焉。牛羊又從而牧之，是以若彼濯濯也。人見其濯濯也，以為未嘗有材焉，此豈山之性也哉？

　　雖存乎人者，豈無仁義之心乎？其所以放其良心者，亦猶斧斤之於木也，旦旦而伐之，可以為美乎？其日夜之所息，平旦之氣，其好惡與人相近也者幾希，則其旦晝之所為，有梏亡之矣。梏之反覆，則其夜氣不足以存。夜氣不足以存，則其違禽獸不遠矣。人見其禽獸也，而以為未嘗有才焉者，是豈人之情也哉！」

郊	*jiāo*	suburb, outskirts of city
斧斤	*fǔ jīn*	axes and adzes
伐	*fá*	chop
息	*xí*	breathe, absorb
潤	*rùn*	moisten, enrich
萌櫱	*méng niè*	sprouts and shoots
牧	*mù*	herd, graze
濯濯	*zhuózhuó*	clean, scoured
旦	*dàn*	morning, dawn
幾希	*jǐxī*	rare
晝	*zhòu*	day time
梏	*gù*	manacle
違	*wéi*	turn against, be apart from
禽獸	*qínshòu*	birds and beasts

Han Yu's Story of the Thousand-Li Horse 韓愈　千里馬

　　世有伯樂，然後有千里馬。千里馬常有，而伯樂不常有。故雖有名馬，只辱於奴隸人之手，駢死於槽櫪之間，不以千里稱之。馬之千里者，一食或盡粟一石。食馬者不知其能千里而食也。是馬也，雖有千里之能，食不飽，力不足，才美不外見。且欲與常馬等不可得，安求其能千里也？策之不以其道，食之不能盡其材，鳴之而不能通其意。執策而臨之曰：「天下無馬。」嗚呼！其真無馬邪？其真不知馬也！

世	*shì*	world, age
伯樂	*Bólè*	a famous trainer of horses
辱	*rǔ*	insult, disgrace
奴隸	*núlì*	slave, servant
駢	*pián*	two horses harnessed together
槽櫪	*cáo lì*	manger and hitching post
稱	*chēng*	call, name
食	*shí*	eat
食	*sì*	feed
粟	*sù*	fodder
石	*dàn*	measure of weight, about 133 lbs.
飽	*bǎo*	full
策	*cè*	whip
執	*zhí*	hold
臨	*lín*	approach
嗚呼	*wūhū*	alas!
邪	*yé*	final particle

Anecdote from *Han Fei Zi*—Mr. He's Jade Disc 韓非子　和氏之璧

　　楚人和氏得玉璞楚山中，奉而獻之厲王。厲王使玉人相之，玉人曰：
「石也。」王以和為誑，刖其左足。及厲王薨，武王即位，和又奉其璞而獻
之武王。武王使玉人相之，又曰：「石也。」王又以和為誑，而刖其右足。
武王薨，文王即位，和乃抱其璞而哭於楚山之下，三日三夜，淚盡而繼之以
血。王聞之，使人問其故曰：「天下之刖者多矣，子希哭之悲也？」和曰：
「吾非悲刖也，悲夫寶玉而題之以石，貞士而名之以誑。此吾所以悲也。」
王乃使玉人理其璞而得寶焉。遂命曰：「和氏之璧。」

璧	*bì*	jade disc used for court rituals
璞	*pú*	uncarved jade
奉	*fèng*	offer
獻	*xiàn*	present gift to a superior
厲王	*Lì Wáng*	King Li
玉人	*yù rén*	jade expert
相	*xiàng*	look at, appraise
誑	*kuáng*	deceive
刖	*yuè*	amputate [as a punishment]
薨	*hōng*	die [said of a ruler]
即位	*jí wèi*	ascend to the throne
繼	*jì*	continue
血	*xuè*	blood
希	*xī*	how? why?
題	*tí*	mention
貞士	*zhēnshì*	upright officer
理	*lǐ*	analyze

Two Tang Lyrics 唐詞

Zhang Ji 張繼　節婦吟

君知妾有夫，贈妾雙明珠，感君纏綿意，系在紅羅襦。

妾家高樓連苑起，良人執戟明光裡。

知君用心如日月，事夫誓擬同生死。

還君明珠雙淚垂，恨不相逢未嫁時。

節	*jié*	chaste, faithful
吟	*yín*	hum, chant; song
妾	*qiè*	concubine; I [woman referring humbly to herself]
贈	*zèng*	give a gift
纏綿	*chánmián*	entwined, tangled
系	*xì*	tie
羅	*luó*	gauze
襦	*rù*	padded jacket
苑	*yuàn*	garden
良人	*liángrén*	good man; my husband
執	*zhí*	carry, hold
戟	*jǐ*	lance, spear
明光	*míngguāng*	name of a hall in the Han palace
誓	*shì*	swear, take an oath
擬	*nǐ*	decide
嫁	*jià*	marry [of a woman]

Liú Yǔxī (772-842) 劉禹錫　春詞

新妝宜面下朱樓，深鎖春光一院愁。

行到中庭數花朵，蜻蜓飛上玉搔頭。

妝	*zhuāng*	adorn, makeup
朱	*zhū*	dark red, vermilion
鎖	*suǒ*	lock
庭	*tíng*	court, hall
朵	*duǒ*	measure word for flowers
蜻蜓	*qīngtíng*	dragonfly
搔頭	*sāotóu*	"scratch-head," a kind of head ornament

Three Regulated Verses 律詩 by Du Fu 杜甫

旅夜書懷

細草微風岸，危檣獨夜舟。星垂平野闊，月涌大江流。

名豈文章著，官因老病休。飄飄何所似？天地一沙鷗。

岸	*àn*	shore
危	*wēi*	steep, leaning
檣	*qiáng*	mast
野	*yě*	wilderness
闊	*kuò*	broad
涌	*yǒng*	well up, rise
著	*zhù*	apparent, famous
飄	*piāo*	float
鷗	*ōu*	seagull

春望

國破山河在，城春草木深。感時花濺淚，恨別鳥驚心。

烽火連三月，家書抵萬金。白頭搔更短，渾欲不勝簪。

濺	*jiàn*	splash
驚	*jīng*	startle
烽	*fēng*	beacon
抵	*dǐ*	substitute; arrive
搔	*sāo*	scratch
渾	*hún*	confused; almost
勝	*shèng*	sustain, hold
簪	*zān*	hair-clasp

江村

清江一曲抱村流，長夏江村事事幽。自去自來堂上燕，相親相近水中鷗。

老妻畫紙為棋局，稚子敲針作釣鉤。多病所須唯藥物，微軀此外更何求？

曲	*qū*	curve, bend
幽	*yōu*	dark, quiet, hidden
堂	*táng*	hall
燕	*yàn*	swallow (bird)
棋局	*qíjú*	chess-board
稚	*zhì*	young
敲	*qiāo*	tap, beat
針	*zhēn*	pin
釣鉤	*diàogōu*	fishhook
軀	*qū*	body

[For Reference—Rough translations of some passages from this lesson]

Mencius—Ox Mountain

Mencius said, "The trees on Ox Mountain used to be beautiful, but since it is on the outskirts of a great kingdom, and people came with axes and adzes to chop them down, how could they continue to be beautiful? Because of the rest [or nourishment] they received every day and night, and the rain and dew that moistened them, shoots and sprouts grew there; but cattle and sheep also grazed on them, and that is why the mountain is so barren today. When people see how barren it is, they think it never had timber growing on it. But how could that be the mountain's original nature?

As for human beings, how could they not have hearts of benevolence and righteousness? Their losing their good hearts is just like the axes and the trees—if you chop away at them every morning, how can they stay beautiful? If, even though one is nourished day and night, and [is under the good influence of] the early morning's air, his likes and dislikes are rarely similar to other people's, this is because what he does during the day serves to manacle and bring him down. If this happens continually, then the night air will not be able to preserve [his good heart]; and if the night air is not able to preserve it, he will be little different from the birds and the beasts. When people see that he is little different from the birds and beasts, they think he never had any talent [or good qualities]. But how could this be man's original nature?"

Du Fu Poems

l)   Fine grass, slight breeze [by the] shore;
        Steep mast, single night boat.
        Stars droop, level wilderness stretches out;
        Moon wells up, great river flows.
        How can fame come from writings?
        I retire from office because of old age and illness.
        Floating, floating, what am I like?
        Heaven earth one sand gull.
              (A sand-gull between heaven and earth? Heaven and earth unites sand and gull?
              One grain-of-sand worth of gull in the universe?)

2)   The nation is broken, but mountains and rivers remain;
The city-wall [bursts forth in] spring, grasses and trees are thick.
Feeling the times, flowers splash tears;
Hating parting, birds startle hearts.
Beacon fires continue three months;
A letter from home is worth ten thousand in gold.
My white hair I scratch even shorter;
It almost won't hold my hair-clasp.

Chengyu

1. 良藥苦口

2. 紙上談兵

3. 微不足道

4. 自力更生

5. 天下無雙

Notes

Lesson 9

Active Vocabulary

醫	*yī*	doctor, heal
聖	*shèng*	sage
盜	*dào*	rob, robber
賊	*zéi*	steal, thief
藏	*cáng*	hide, conceal
眾	*zhòng*	crowd, multitude
立	*lì*	stand
結	*jié*	tie, contract; construct
夕	*xī*	evening
徒	*tú*	only, merely
舞	*wǔ*	dance
醒	*xǐng*	awake, sober
醉	*zuì*	drunk
交	*jiāo*	join, mutual
散	*sàn*	disperse
永	*yǒng*	eternal
了	*liǎo*	finish
朱	*zhū*	vermilion, red
向	*xiàng*	toward
異	*yì*	different
悲	*bēi*	sorrow; tragic

From Mo Zi 墨子 (5th cent. B.C.) On Universal Love 兼愛

聖人以治天下為事者也，必知亂之所自起，焉能治之。不知亂之所自起，則不能治。譬之如醫之攻人之疾者然，必知疾之所自起，焉能攻之。不知疾之所自起，則弗能攻。治亂者何獨不然？必知亂之所自起，焉能治之。不知亂之所自起，則弗能治。聖人以治天下為事者也，不可不查亂之所自起。

當查亂何自起，起不相愛。臣子之不孝君父，所謂亂也。子自愛，不愛父，故虧父而自利。弟自愛，不愛兄，故虧兄而自利。臣自愛，不愛君，故虧君而自利。此所謂亂也。雖父之不慈子，兄之不慈弟，君之不慈臣，此亦天下之所謂亂也。父自愛也，不愛子，故虧子而自利。兄自愛也，不愛弟，故虧弟而自利。君自愛也，不愛臣，故虧臣而自利。是何也？皆起不相愛。

…若使天下兼相愛，國與國不相攻，家與家不相亂，盜賊亡有，君臣父子皆能孝慈，若此，則天下治。故聖人以治天下為事者，惡得不禁惡而勸愛？故天下兼相愛則治，交相惡則亂。故子墨子曰：「不可以不勸愛人」者，此也。

兼	*jiān*	together, equal
譬	*pì*	compare
疾	*jí*	illness
查	*chá*	examine
虧	*kuī*	lose; injure
慈	*cí*	kind, compassionate
亡	*(here) wú*	同無
惡	*wū*	how?
禁	*jìn*	prohibit
惡	*wù*	hate
勸	*quàn*	urge, pursuade

From Sun Zi's *Art of War* 孫子兵法

　　孫子曰：昔之善戰者，先為不可勝，以待敵之可勝。不可勝在己，可勝在敵。故善戰者，能為不可勝，不能使敵必可勝。故曰：勝可知而不可為。

　　不可勝者，守也。可勝者，攻也。守則不足，攻則有餘。善守者，藏於九地之下。善攻者，動於九天之上。故能自保而全勝也。

　　見勝，不過眾人之所知，非善之善者也。戰勝，而天下曰善，非善之善者也。故舉秋毫，不為多力。見日月，不為明目。聞雷霆，不為聰耳。古之善戰者，勝於易勝者也。故善戰者之勝也，無智名，無勇功。故其戰勝不忒，不忒者，其措必勝，勝已敗者也。故善戰者，立於不敗之地，而不失敵之敗也。是故勝兵先勝，而後求戰。敗兵先戰，而後求勝。

待	*dài*	wait for
守	*shǒu*	guard, protect
保	*bǎo*	protect, preserve
秋毫	*qiūháo*	"autumn down," i.e., small and light
雷霆	*léitíng*	thunder
聰	*cōng*	clever, acute
功	*gōng*	achievement
忒	*tè*	fault, mistake
措	*cuò*	arrange, take measures

Poem by Tao Qian 陶潛　　飲酒

結廬在人境，而無事馬喧。問君何能爾，心遠地自偏。

采菊東籬下，悠然見南山。山氣日夕佳，飛鳥相與還。

此中有真意，欲辯已忘言。

廬	*lú*	hut
境	*jìng*	border, edge
喧	*xuān*	noise
爾	*ěr*	thus, so
偏	*piān*	one-sided, leaning
采	*cǎi*	pluck, gather
菊	*jú*	chrysanthemum
籬	*lí*	fence
悠	*yōu*	distant
佳	*jīa*	good, excellent
辯	*biàn*	discuss

Song 曲 by Ma Zhiyuan 馬致遠 (fl. 1300) 天淨沙　秋思

(This poem is a *qǔ* 曲 (song) from the Yuan dyansty. The first part of the title is the name of the tune; the second part is the name of this particular poem. The poem is famous for evoking a landscape with a series of visual images, using very few verbs.)

枯藤　老樹　昏鴉。　小橋　流水　平沙。　古道　西風　瘦馬。

夕陽西下。　斷腸人在天涯。

枯	*kū*	withered
藤	*téng*	vine
昏	*hūn*	evening, dusk
鴉	*yā*	crow
斷	*duàn*	sever
腸	*cháng*	internal organs
	斷腸	heartbroken
涯	*yá*	horizon

Poem by Li Bai 李白　月下獨酌

花間一壺酒，獨酌無相親。舉杯邀明月，對影成三人。

月既不解酒，影徒隨我身。暫伴月將影，行樂須及春。

我歌月徘徊，我舞影零亂。醒時同交歡，醉後各分散。

永結無情遊，相期邈雲漢。

酌	*zhuó*	pour wine
壺	*hú*	pot
邀	*yāo*	invite
隨	*suí*	follow
暫	*zhàn*	temporarily
伴	*bàn*	companion
徘徊	*páihuái*	waver
零亂	*língluàn*	in confusion
期	*qī*	set a date
邈	*miǎo*	distant
雲漢	*yúnhàn*	"cloudy Han [river]"=Milky Way

Lyric 詞 by Li Yu 李煜　(tune title 虞美人)

春花秋月何時了？往時知多少？小樓昨夜又東風，故國不堪回首月明中。

雕欄玉砌依然在，只是朱顏改。問君能有幾多愁，恰是一江春水向東流。

虞	*yú*	(surname)
往	*wǎng*	go; past
堪	*kān*	bear
雕	*diāo*	carved
欄	*lán*	railings
砌	*qì*	stairs, steps
依然	*yīrán*	as before
顏	*yán*	face
恰	*qià*	exactly

Yanzi Serves as Ambassador to Chu (II) 晏子將使楚

晏子將使楚。楚王聞之，謂左右曰：「晏嬰齊之習辭令者也。今方來，吾欲辱之。何以也？」左右對曰：「為其來也，臣請縛一人，過王而行。王曰：『何為者也？』對曰：『齊人也。』王曰：『何坐？』曰：『坐盜。』」

晏子至，楚王賜晏子酒。酒酣，吏二縛一人詣王。王曰：「縛者曷為者也？」對曰：「齊人也，坐盜。」王視晏子曰：「齊人固善盜乎？」

晏子避席對曰：「嬰聞之，橘生淮南則為橘，生於淮北則為枳。葉徒相似，其實味不同。所以然者何？水土異也。今民生於齊不盜，入楚則盜，得無楚之水土使民善盜耶？」

王笑曰：「聖人非所與熙也，寡人反取病焉。」

嬰	*yīng*	Yanzi's name
習	*xí*	practiced
辭令	*cílìng*	clever speech
辱	*rǔ*	insult
縛	*fù*	tie up
坐	*zuò*	(here) be accused
賜	*cì*	bestow
酣	*hān*	partly drunk
吏	*lì*	official
詣	*yì*	go to visit
曷	*hé*	何
避	*bì*	leave
席	*xí*	mat, banquet seat
橘	*jú*	sweet orange
淮	*Huái*	name of a river
枳	*zhǐ*	bitter orange
葉	*yè*	leaves
味	*wèi*	flavor
耶	*yé*	final particle
熙	*xī*	mock, trick
寡人	*guǎrén*	ruler's way of referring to himself

Lyric 詞 by Su Shi　蘇軾 (1037-1101)　水調歌頭

明月幾時有？把酒問青天。不知天上宮闕，今夕是何年？

我欲乘風歸去，又恐瓊樓玉宇，高處不勝寒。

起舞弄清影，何似在人間？

轉朱閣，低綺戶，照無眠。不應有恨，何事長向別時圓？

人有悲歡離合，月有陰晴圓缺，此事古難全。

但願人長久，千里共嬋娟。

調	*diào*	tune
宮	*gōng*	palace
闕	*quē*	pavilion
乘	*chéng*	ride on
瓊	*qióng*	precious jade
宇	*yǔ*	chamber
弄	*nòng*	play with
閣	*gé*	room, building
綺	*qǐ*	gauze
眠	*mián*	sleep
晴	*qíng*	clear, bright
缺	*quē*	lacking
共	*gòng*	together, share
嬋娟	*chánjuān*	lovely (moon)

From Sun Zi's *Art of War* (Ch. 4)

Sunzi said, "Those skilled in the art of war in former times first made certain they could not be conquered, and then waited for a time when the enemy could be conquered. Not being conquered is something one can control oneself; being vulnerable to being conquered is something that depends on the enemy. Thus the good warrior can make himself unconquerable, but can not make the enemy conquerable. Therefore it is said, 'One can know who will conquer, but one can not force a conquest.'

The way to keep from being conquered is to protect oneself. The way to conquer is to attack. Protecting oneself is not enough [to defeat another]; by attacking one may go too far [and make oneself vulnerable]. Those good at protecting themselves hide under the nine-layered earth. Those good at attacking move from above the nine-layered heavens. Therefore they can protect themselves and assure complete victory.

When you observe a victory, it is only what the masses can know; it is not the best of the best. When there is a victory in battle and everyone says, "Wonderful!" it is not the best of the best. It does not take much strength to lift an autumn feather; it does not take keen eyesight to see the sun and moon; it does not take acute hearing to detect thunder. The ancients who were good at fighting conquered those who were easy to conquer; therefore they did not win fame for being clever, or merit for being brave. Now those who win do so by making no mistakes. Those who make no mistakes will win; they will conquer one who is already defeated. Thus the one good at fighting stands on undefeatable ground, and from there he will not lose his enemy's defeat. For this reason, the victorious army first secures its victory and then seeks battle, while the losing army first fights and then seeks victory."

Poem by Li Bai

A pot of wine amid the flowers; I pour it out alone, with no companions.
I raise my cup and invite the bright moon; with it and my shadow we have become three persons.
The moon does not understand how to drink, and my shadow only follows my body.
For the moment the moon and my shadow are my companions;
     we must take advantage of springtime to enjoy ourselves.
I sing and the moon wavers back and forth, I dance and my shadow moves about in confusion.
While we are sober we enjoy each other; when drunk we part company.
Let's make an eternal pact as emotion-less wanderers, to meet each other at the distant Milky Way.

Poem by Su Shi

How long has the bright moon existed? I raise my wine[cup] and ask the blue sky.
I wonder what year this is in the palaces of heaven [on the moon]?
I want to ride the wind and return there, but I'm afraid that in those jasper towers and jade halls
     it would be unbearably cold.
So I arise and dance with my clear shadow, isn't it better in the world of men?
Turning among the vermilion buildings, under the gauze door, shining on the sleepless ones.
You [i.e., the moon, to whom the poet is speaking]should not have anything against me,
     so why are you always so round at times of parting?
People have their sorrows and joys, their separations and reunions;
The moon has its darkness and light, its fullness and lack thereof; this has never come to an end.
I only wish we could live a long time, and that together we could enjoy the lovely [moon],
     though we are a thousand *li* apart.

Chengyu:

1. 不了了之

2. 大同小異

3. 大事化小，小事化了

4. 悲歡離合

5. 朝發夕至

Notes

Lesson 10

Active Vocabulary

娶	*qǔ*	take as a wife
貧	*pín*	poor
收	*shōu*	collect, accept
持	*chí*	carry, take
即	*jí*	then; if
洗	*xǐ*	wash, bathe
共	*gòng*	together
逃	*táo*	escape, flee
投	*tóu*	throw
煩	*fán*	trouble, bother
報	*bào*	report
送	*sòng*	send off
驚	*jīng*	startle
留	*liú*	keep, stay
孫	*sūn*	grandchild
慮	*lǜ*	worry
患	*huàn*	suffer, worry
箭	*jiàn*	arrow
軍	*jūn*	army, troops
殺	*shā*	kill
代	*dài*	substitute
便	*biàn*	then; convenient
辦	*bàn*	do, take care of

弄	*nòng*	use, play with
被	*bèi*	indicates passive
肯	*kěn*	willing
換	*huàn*	substitute
把	*bǎ*	take
害	*hài*	harm
勸	*quàn*	urge, pursuade
次	*cì*	second, next; a time
誤	*wù*	mistake
戲	*xì*	play, joke
救	*jiù*	save, rescue
船	*chuán*	boat
快	*kuài*	fast
滿	*mǎn*	full

Shi Ji 史記 or *Records of the Historian*

The first passage in this lesson is taken from China's great historical work, the *Shi Ji* 史記 or *Records of the Historian*, by Sīmǎ Qiān 司馬遷 (145?-90? B.C.), of the Former Han dynasty. Sima Qian's monumental work, in 130 chapters, is the first of the official dynastic histories, and it set the standard for subsequent dynastic histories. It is divided into five sections: Basic Annals [of ruling houses], Chronological Tables, Treatises [on subjects such as rivers, astronomy, rites, and music], Hereditary Houses [accounts of feudal families], and Biographies. The story below comes from the Biographies 傳 section.

史記　　西門豹治鄴

　　魏文侯時，西門豹為鄴令。豹往到鄴，會長老，問之民所疾苦。長老曰：「苦為河伯娶婦，以故貧。」

　　豹問其故。對曰：「鄴三老，廷掾，常歲賦斂百姓，收取其錢，得數百萬，用其二三十萬為河伯娶婦，與祝巫共分其餘錢，持歸。

　　「當其時，巫行視人家女好者，云：『是當為河伯婦。』即聘取，洗沐之，為治新繒綺縠衣，間居齋戒。為治齋宮河上，張緹絳帷，女居其中。為具牛、酒、飯食。行十餘日，共粉飾之，如嫁女床席，令女居其上，浮之河中。始浮，行數十里，乃沒。

　　「其人家有好女者，恐大巫祝為河伯娶之，以故多持女遠逃亡。以故城中益空無人，又困貧。所從來久遠矣。民人俗語曰：『即不為河伯娶婦，水來漂沒，溺其人民云』。」

　　西門豹曰：「至為河伯娶婦時，願三老，巫祝，父老送女河上，幸來告語之，吾亦往送女！」

　　皆曰：「諾！」

　　至其時，西門豹往會之河上。三老，官屬，豪長者，里父老皆會。以人民往觀之者三二千人。其巫，老女子也，已年七十，從弟子女十人所，皆衣繒單衣，立大巫後。

　　西門豹曰：「呼河伯婦來，視其好醜！」

即將女出帷中，來至前。豹視之，顧謂三老，巫祝，父老曰：
「是女子不好，煩大巫嫗為人報河伯：得更求好女，後日送之。」即使吏卒
共抱大巫嫗，投之河中。

有頃，曰：「巫嫗何久也？弟子趣之！」後以弟子一人投河中。

有頃，曰：「弟子何久也？復使一人趣之！」復投一弟子河中。凡投
之三子。

西門豹曰：「巫嫗，弟子，是女子也，不能白事。煩三老為入白之！」
復投三老河中。

西門豹簪筆，磬折，向河立待良久。長老，吏，傍觀者皆驚恐。

西門豹顧曰：「巫嫗，三老不來還，奈之何？」欲復使廷掾與豪長
者一人入趣之。皆叩頭，叩頭且破額，血流地，色如死灰。

西門豹曰：「諾！且留！待之須臾。」

須臾，豹曰：「廷掾起矣！狀河伯留客之久，若皆罷去，歸矣！」鄴
吏民大驚恐。從是以後，不敢復言為河伯娶婦。

西門豹即發民鑿十二渠，引河水灌民田，田皆溉。

當其時，民治渠少煩苦，不欲也。豹曰：「民可與樂成，不可與慮始。
今父老子弟雖患苦我，然百歲後，期令父老子孫思我言！」

至今皆得水利，民人以給足富。

Supplementary Vocabulary

西門豹	*Xīmén Bào*	人名
鄴	*yè*	地名
魏文侯	*Wèi Wén Hóu*	人名，Duke Wen of Wei
令	*lìng*	prefect
長老	*zhǎng lǎo*	elders
疾苦	*jíkǔ*	suffering
河伯	*Hé Bó*	Lord of the [Yellow] River
廷掾	*tíngyuàn*	minor bureaucrats
賦斂	*fùliǎn*	impose taxes
巫／祝巫／巫祝	*wū/zhùwū/wūzhù*	shaman, shamaness
云	*yún*	say
聘	*pìn*	engage (to marry)
沐	*mù*	wash hair
繒	*zēng*	thick silk
綺	*qǐ*	patterned silk
縠	*hú*	crinkled silk
齋戒	*zhāijiè*	fast (not eat)
齋宮	*zhāigōng*	shrine
緹	*tí*	yellow
絳	*jiàng*	red
帷	*wéi*	curtain
具	*jù*	prepare
粉飾	*fěnshì*	powder and adorn
嫁	*jià*	marry
席	*xí*	mat
沒	*mò*	sink

益	*yì*	more
困	*kùn*	difficult
漂沒	*piāomò*	float and sink
溺	*nì*	drown
幸	*xìng*	hope, would you please
諾	*nuò*	yes
官屬	*guānshǔ*	officials and staff
豪	*háo*	powerful families
里	*lǐ*	village
弟子	*dìzǐ*	disciples
單	*dān*	single-layered
醜	*chǒu*	ugly
顧	*gù*	look back at
巫嫗	*wūyù*	witch
吏卒	*lìzú*	officers
頃	*qǐng*	short while
趣	*cù*	urge on
白	*bái*	explain
簪筆	*zānbǐ*	thrust pen behind ear
磬折	*qìngzhé*	bow
待	*dài*	wait
傍	*páng*	side
奈之何	*nàizhīhé*	what can be done?
叩頭	*kòutóu*	kowtow
額	*é*	brow
血	*xuè*	blood
灰	*huī*	ashes

須臾	*xūyú*	short time
狀	*zhuàng*	appear
罷	*bà*	quit, rest
發	*fā*	send out
鑿	*záo*	dig
渠	*qú*	ditch, channel
灌	*guàn*	irrigate
溉	*gài*	pour in
期	*qī*	hope, expect

Romance of the Three Kingdoms 三國志演義

The final text in this lesson is a famous incident from *The Romance of the Three Kingdoms* 三國志演義, China's most popular historical novel. The novel is based on the official history of the Three Kingdoms period (184-280 A.D.); the present fictional version is ascribed to Luó Guànzhōng 羅貫中 of the fourteenth century, with revisions by later scholars. The language is largely classical, but it also contains elements of modern *báihuà*.

Background for the story: The protagonist is Zhūgě Liàng 諸葛亮, also known by his courtesy name Kǒngmíng 孔明. He is a brilliant strategist, working at this point for Zhōu Yú 周瑜 (also known as Gōngjǐn 公瑾), whose troops are camped east of the river 江東. Zhou Yu feels threatened by the brilliance of his strategist, and would like to get rid of him. Lǔ Sù 魯肅 (Zǐjìng 子敬) is also under Zhou Yu's command, and he serves as an intermediary between Zhuge Liang and Zhou Yu in this story. Their main opponent is Cáo Cāo 曹操, who is camped with his troops across the river.

The first paragraph in this passage notes that Cao Cao has been tricked by Zhou Yu into killing two of his naval commanders. Zhou Yu is pleased to receive the report of his plan's success, and wants to find out if Zhuge Liang knows anything about it.

Names that occur in this excerpt:

諸葛亮	*Zhūgě Liàng* (孔明 *Kǒngmíng*)	strategist for Zhou Yu
周瑜	*Zhōu Yú* (公瑾 *Gōngjǐn*)	leader of the 江東 troops
魯肅	*Lǔ Sù* (子敬 *Zǐjìng*)	officer under Zhou Yu
曹操	*Cáo Cāo*	leader of the enemy troops
蔡瑁	*Cài Mào*	officer under Cao Cao
張允	*Zhāng Yǔn*	officer under Cao Cao
毛玠	*Máo Jiè*	officer under Cao Cao
于禁	*Yú Jìn*	officer under Cao Cao
蔣干	*Jiǎng Gàn*	officer under Cao Cao
張遼	*Zhāng Liáo*	officer under Cao Cao
徐晃	*Xú Huàng*	officer under Cao Cao

三國志演義　　孔明借箭

　　　話説曹操駐軍三江口，中了周瑜之計，殺卻水軍都督蔡瑁、張允二人，於眾將內選毛玠、于禁為水軍都督，以代蔡、張二人之職。細作探知，報過江東。周瑜大喜曰：「吾所患者，此二人耳，今既勦除。吾不憂矣。」魯肅曰：「都督用兵如此，何愁曹賊不破乎。」瑜曰：「吾料諸將不知此計，只有諸葛亮識見勝我，想此謀亦不能瞞也。子敬試以言挑之，看他知也不知，便當回報。」

　　　魯肅領了周瑜言語，徑來舟中相探孔明。孔明接入小舟對坐。肅曰：「連日措辦軍物，有失聽教。」孔明曰：「便是亮亦未與都督賀喜。」肅曰：「何喜？」孔明曰：「公瑾使先生來探亮知也不知，便是這件事可賀喜耳。」嚇得魯肅也失色，問曰：「先生何由知之？」孔明曰：「這條計只好弄蔣干。曹操雖被一時瞞過，必然便省悟，只是不肯認錯，今蔡、張兩人既死，江東無患矣，如何不賀喜？吾聞曹操換毛玠、于禁為水軍都督，則在這兩個手裡，好歹送了水軍性命。」魯肅聽了，開口不得，把言語支吾了半晌，別孔明而回。孔明囑曰：「望子敬在公瑾面前勿言亮先知此事。恐公瑾心懷妒忌，又要尋事害亮。」

　　　魯肅應諾而去，回見周瑜。把上項只得實説了。瑜大驚曰：「此人決不可留。吾決意斬之。」魯肅曰：「若殺孔明，卻被曹操笑也。」瑜曰：「吾自有公道斬之。教他死而無怨。」肅曰：「以何公道斬之？」瑜曰：「子敬休問，來日便見。」

　　　次日，聚眾將於帳下，教請孔明議事。孔明欣然而至。坐定，瑜問孔明曰：「即日將與曹軍交戰，水路交兵，當以何兵器為先？」孔明曰：「大江之上，以弓箭為先。」瑜曰：「先生之言甚合愚意。但今軍中正缺箭用，敢煩先生監造十萬枝箭，以為應敵之具。此系公事，先生幸勿推卻。」孔明曰：「都督見委，自當效勞。敢問十萬枝箭，何時要用？」瑜曰：「十日之內完辦否？」孔明曰：「曹軍即日將至，若候十日，必誤大事。」瑜曰：

「先生料幾日可完辦?」孔明曰:「只消三日,便可拜納十萬枝箭。」瑜曰:「軍中無戲言!」孔明曰:「怎敢戲都督?願納軍令狀,三日不辦,甘當重罰。」瑜大喜,喚軍政司當面取了文書,置酒相待,曰:「待軍事畢後,自有酬勞。」孔明曰:「今日已不及,來日造起,至第三日,可差五百小軍到江邊搬箭。」飲了數杯,辭去。

魯肅曰:「此人莫非詐乎?」瑜曰:「他自送死,非我逼他。今明自對眾要了文書,他便兩脅生翅,也飛不去。我只分付軍匠人等,教他故意遲延,凡應物件都不與齊備。如此,必然誤了日期。那時定罪,有何可說?今公可去探他虛實,卻來回報。」

肅領命來見孔明。孔明曰:「我曾告子敬,休對公瑾說,他必要害我。不想子敬不肯為我隱諱,今日果然又弄出事來。三日內如何造得十萬箭?子敬只得救我!」肅曰:「公自取其禍,我如何救得你?」孔明曰:「望子敬借我二十只船,每只要軍士三十人,船上皆用青布為幔,各束草千餘個,分布兩邊。吾別有妙用。第三日,包管有十萬枝箭。只不可又教公瑾得知。若彼知之,吾計敗矣!」

肅允諾,卻不解其意,回報周瑜,果然不提起借船之事,只言孔明并不用箭竹、翎毛膠漆等物,自有道理。瑜大疑曰:「且看三日後如何,回報我。」

卻說魯肅私自撥輕快船二十只,各船三十餘人,并布幔束草等物,盡皆齊備,候孔明調用。第一日,卻不見孔明動靜。第二日,亦只不動。第三日四更時分,孔明密請魯肅到船中。肅問曰:「公召我來何意?」孔明曰:「特請子敬同往取箭。」肅曰:「何處去取?」孔明曰:「子敬休問,前去便見。」遂命將二十只船用長索相連,徑望北岸進發。是夜大霧漫天,長江之中,霧氣更甚,對面不相見,孔明促舟前進。

當夜五更時候,船已近曹操水寨。孔明教把船只頭西,尾東,一帶擺開,就船上擂鼓吶喊。魯肅驚曰:「倘曹兵齊出,如之奈何?」孔明笑曰:「吾料曹操不敢輕出。吾等只顧酌酒取樂,待霧散便回。」

卻説曹操寨中聽得擂鼓吶喊，毛玠、于禁二人慌忙飛報曹操。操傳令曰：「重霧迷江，彼軍忽至，必有埋伏，切不可輕動。可撥水軍弓弩手亂箭射之。」又差人往旱寨內喚張遼、徐晃各帶弓弩軍三千，火速到江邊助射。比及號令到來，毛玠、于禁怕南軍搶入水寨，已差弓弩手在寨前放箭。少項，旱寨弓弩手亦到，約一萬餘人，盡皆向江中放箭，箭如雨發。孔明教把船吊回，頭東尾西，逼近水寨收箭。一面擂鼓吶喊。待至日高霧散，孔明令收船急回。二十只船兩邊束草上，排滿箭枝。孔明令各船上軍士齊聲叫約：「謝丞相箭！」比及曹軍寨內報知曹操時，這裡船輕水急，已放回二十餘里，追之不及。曹操懊悔不已。

　　卻説孔明回船，謂魯肅曰：「每船上箭約五六千矣，不費江東半分之力，已得十萬餘箭。明日，即將來射曹軍，卻不甚便？」魯肅拜服。

　　船到岸時，周瑜已差五百軍在江邊等候搬箭。孔明教於船上取之，可得十萬餘枝，都搬入中軍帳交納。魯肅入見周瑜，備説孔明取箭之事。瑜大驚，慨然嘆曰：「孔明神機妙算，吾不如也。」

Supplementary Vocabulary for *Three Kingdoms* selection

三國志演義 *Sān Guó Zhì Yǎnyì*   *Romance of the Three Kingdoms*
(also 三國演義 *Sān Guó Yǎnyì*)

駐	zhù	be stationed at		半晌	bànshǎng	a short while
三江口	Sān Jiāng Kǒu	place name		囑	zhǔ	order
中…計	zhòng…jì	fall for a plot		妒忌	dùjì	jealous, envious
都督	dūdū	commander		尋	xún	seek
職	zhí	official post, job		應諾	yìngnuò	agree
探	tàn	investigate		項	xiàng	event, item
耳	ěr	而已		斬	zhǎn	execute
勦除	chāochú	get rid of		怨	yuàn	complain; complaint
憂	yōu	worry		聚	jù	assemble
料	liào	think, imagine		帳	zhàng	tent
識見	shíjiàn	understanding		議	yì	discuss
瞞	mán	deceive		欣然	xīnrán	happy
挑	tiǎo	tease, provoke		弓	gōng	bow
領	lǐng	receive an order		愚	yú	foolish, my [humble]
徑	jìng	go directly		缺	quē	lack
接	jiē	accept		監	jiān	supervise
措	cuò	arrange, take measures		造	zào	manufacture
賀喜	hèxǐ	congratulate		枝	zhī	measure for arrows
嚇	xià	afraid		具	jù	implement
條	tiáo	measure word for plans		系	xì	is
省悟	xǐngwù	become aware		推卻	tuīquè	decline
認錯	rèncuò	admit a mistake		委	wěi	commission
好歹	hǎodǎi	good or bad, in any case		效勞	xiàoláo	carry out work effectively
支吾	zhīwú	hesitate				

候	*hòu*	wait		隱諱	*yǐnhuì*	conceal
消	*xiāo*	melt, dissolve		禍	*huò*	disaster
拜納	*bàinà*	offer		只	*zhī*	measure for boats
怎	*zěn*	how?		士	*shì*	gentlemen, officers, soldiers
令狀	*lǐngzhuàng*	written orders		布	*bù*	cloth
罰	*fá*	penalty		幔	*màn*	curtain, cover
喚	*huàn*	call		束	*shù*	bundle
司	*sī*	control		妙	*miào*	wonderful, clever
置	*zhì*	set up, lay out		包管	*bāoguǎn*	guarantee
待	*dài*	treat		允諾	*yǔnnuò*	agree
畢	*bì*	finish		解	*jiě*	understand
酬勞	*chóuláo*	reward		果然	*guǒrán*	actually
差	*chāi*	dispatch, send		提	*tí*	bring up
搬	*bān*	move, transport		竹	*zhú*	bamboo
詐	*zhà*	falsehood		翎毛	*língmáo*	feathers
逼	*bī*	force		膠	*jiāo*	glue
脅	*xié*	shoulder		漆	*qī*	lacquer, varnish
翅	*chì*	wing		道理	*dàolǐ*	reason
分付	*fēnfù*	order		私	*sī*	privately
匠	*jiàng*	craftsmen		撥	*bō*	bring out
故意	*gùyì*	deliberately		調	*diào*	deploy
遲延	*chíyán*	delay		更	*gēng*	watch (one-fifth of the night)
件	*jiàn*	measure for things		密	*mì*	secretly
齊備	*qíbèi*	all ready		召	*zhào*	summon
期	*qī*	date		特	*tè*	special, especially
罪	*zuì*	crime, fault		索	*suǒ*	rope
公	*gōng*	you, sir		岸	*àn*	shore, bank
曾	*céng*	indicates action in the past				

漫	*màn*	overflow		約	*yuē*	approximately
促	*cù*	urge		發	*fā*	emit
寨	*zhài*	camp		吊	*diào*	hang, draw back
尾	*wěi*	tail		急	*jí*	urgent
帶	*dài*	string, belt		排	*pái*	arrange
擺	*bǎi*	set out		丞相	*chéngxiàng*	prime minister
擂鼓	*léigǔ*	beat drums		追	*zhuī*	pursue
吶喊	*nàhǎn*	give a battle-cry		懊悔	*aòhuǐ*	irritated
倘	*tǎng*	if		費	*fèi*	spend, waste
齊	*qí*	all together		拜服	*bàifú*	bow, pay respects
拉何	*nàihé*	how?		慨然	*kǎirán*	magnanimously
吾等	*wúděng*	we		嘆	*tàn*	sigh
顧	*gù*	pay attention to, worry about		神機	*shénjī*	divine plan
酌	*zhuó*	pour wine		妙算	*miàosuàn*	wonderful calculation
樂	*lè*	entertainment				
慌忙	*huāngmáng*	hurriedly				
迷	*mí*	obscure				
埋伏	*máifu*	ambush				
切	*qiè*	definitely				
弓弩手	*gōngnǔshǒu*	archers				
射	*shè*	shoot				
旱	*hàn*	dry land				
速	*sù*	quickly				
比及	*bǐjí*	when				
號令	*hàolìng*	order				
搶	*qiǎng*	take by force				
少項	*shǎoqǐng*	after a moment				

Chengyu

1. 小巫見大巫

2. 謀事在人，成事在天

3. 驚天動地

4. 說曹操，曹操就到

5. 三個臭皮匠，合成一個諸葛亮

   (臭 *chòu*—stink; 皮匠 *píjiàng*—cobbler)

Notes

Active Vocabulary

(Active Vocabulary, Lessons 1-10. Number in parentheses after each item is Lesson number.)

安	*ān*	how? where? (5)
把	*bǎ*	take (10)
敗	*bài*	defeat; be defeated (7)
辦	*bàn*	do, take care of (10)
抱	*bào*	embrace, hold close to chest (8)
報	*bào*	report (10)
被	*bèi*	indicates passive (10)
悲	*bēi*	sorrow; tragic (9)
彼	*bǐ*	that (7)
便	*biàn*	then; convenient (10)
別	*bié*	separate, be apart (5)
才	*cái*	talent (8)
材	*cái*	timber, material (8)
殘	*cán*	leftover, injured (7)
藏	*cáng*	hide, conceal (9)
嘗	*cháng*	taste; indicates action in the past (8)
塵	*chén*	dust (7)
臣	*chén*	minister; government servant; I, your servant (3)
誠	*chéng*	sincere; sincerity (3)
持	*chí*	carry, take (10)
愁	*chóu*	feel sad (6)
初	*chū*	first, beginning (5)
船	*chuán*	boat (10)
垂	*chuí*	hang down (8)
次	*cì*	second, next; a time (10)
此	*cǐ*	this, these (3)
詞	*cí*	words, lyrics (8)
存	*cún*	exist, live (6)
代	*dài*	substitute (10)
但	*dàn*	only (3)
當	*dāng*	suitable, ought; now, at the time (7)
道	*dào*	path; the Way; to say (2)
盜	*dào*	rob, robber (9)
德	*dé*	virtue, moral power (3)
等	*děng*	compare, equal (8)
斷	*duàn*	cut short, break off (6)
對	*duì*	face toward, reply (7)

而	*ér*	and, but (2)	
而已	*éryǐ*	that is all (5)	
法	*fǎ*	law, method (6)	
凡	*fán*	all (7)	
煩	*fán*	trouble, bother (10)	
放	*fàng*	let go (6)	
方	*fāng*	when, then (7)	
逢	*féng*	meet, encounter (8)	
否	*fǒu*	or not (7)	
復	*fù*	again; return; repeat (3)	
浮	*fú*	float (5)	
夫	*fū*	man, husband (6)	
夫	*fù*	introductory particle (6)	
弗	*fú*	not + him/her/it (4)	
婦	*fù*	woman (8)	
感	*gǎn*	feelings, emotion (6)	
更	*gèng*	change; even more, once more (8)	
攻	*gōng*	attack (8)	
共	*gòng*	together (10)	
固	*gù*	strong, rigid; definitely (5)	
故	*gù*	therefore (8)	
害	*hài*	harm (10)	
寒	*hán*	cold (7)	
何	*hé*	what? how? (4)	
乎	*hū*	final particle indicating question or exclamation (6)	
忽	*hū*	suddenly (5)	
化	*huà*	change, transform (6)	
懷	*huái*	think about, remember fondly; embrace (2)	
換	*huàn*	substitute (10)	
患	*huàn*	suffer, worry (10)	
或	*huò*	someone; perhaps (4)	
既	*jì*	already, since (5)	
及	*jí*	arrive at, when; as well as (4)	
即	*jí*	be the same as (3)	
即	*jí*	then, if (10)	
箭	*jiàn*	arrow (10)	
將	*jiàng*	general in the army (6)	
將	*jiāng*	lead; take; indicates future (6)	
講	*jiǎng*	talk, discuss (7)	
交	*jiāo*	join, mutual (9)	
皆	*jiē*	all (2)	
結	*jié*	tie, contract; construct (9)	
盡	*jìn*	disappear, exhaust (6)	
經	*jīng*	pass through, experience; classic, scripture (5)	

驚	*jīng*	startle (10)
就	*jiù*	go toward (6)
久	*jiǔ*	long time (5)
救	*jiù*	save, rescue (10)
絕	*jué*	cut off, end, extreme (6)
軍	*jūn*	army, troops (10)
君	*jūn*	lord; you (2)
君子	*jūnzǐ*	gentleman (2)
肯	*kěn*	willing (10)
恐	*kǒng*	fear (7)
快	*kuài*	fast (10)
樂	*lè*	joy (6)
淚	*lèi*	tears (7)
立	*lì*	stand (9)
理	*lǐ*	structure; reason; principle (6)
連	*lián*	connect, connected, one after another (8)
良	*liáng*	good (8)
良心	*liángxīn*	conscience (8)
了	*liǎo*	finish (9)
鄰	*lín*	neighbor (7)
令	*lìng*	order, cause (5)
留	*liú*	keep, stay (10)
慮	*lù*	worry (10)
滿	*mǎn*	full (10)
矛	*máo*	spear (4)
苗	*miáo*	sprouts (4)
鳴	*míng*	call of a bird or other animal (8)
命	*mìng*	command; fate (2)
莫	*mò*	none, not (4)
乃	*nǎi*	then, only then; be (4)
寧	*níng*	rather (4)
弄	*nòng*	use, play with (10)
篇	*piān*	section of a book (7)
貧	*pín*	poor (10)
其	*qí*	his, her, its; this, that (2)
豈	*qǐ*	how can it be? (6)
器	*qì*	utensil, vessel (7)
妻	*qī*	wife (8)
且	*qiě*	moreover (5)
求	*qiú*	seek (6)
娶	*qǔ*	take as a wife (10)
勸	*quàn*	urge, pursuade (10)
卻	*què*	however (7)
群	*qún*	flock, group, crowd (7)

然		*rán*	yes, thus; but (4)
仁		*rén*	humane-ness, benevolence (3)
容易		*róngyì*	easy (5)
若		*ruò*	if; like (3)
散		*sàn*	disperse (9)
殺		*shā*	kill (10)
沙		*shā*	sand (8)
尚		*shàng*	still (7)
舌		*shé*	tongue (4)
勝		*shèng*	overcome, conquer (5)
聖		*shèng*	sage (9)
使		*shǐ*	cause, let, allow; if (6)
氏		*shì*	clan, surname, Mr./Ms. (8)
收		*shōu*	collect, accept (10)
暑		*shǔ*	hot (7)
雙		*shuāng*	pair (8)
似		*sì*	be like, resemble (2)
送		*sòng*	send off (10)
俗		*sú*	custom; common, ordinary (6)
遂		*suì*	follow, after that, then (4)
孫		*sūn*	grandchild (10)
所		*suǒ*	place; that which (3)
他，它		*tā*	other (6)
逃		*táo*	escape, flee (10)
桃		*táo*	peach (6)
添		*tiān*	add (5)
投		*tóu*	throw (10)
徒		*tú*	only, merely (9)
亡		*wáng*	lose, decline, die (6)
為		*wéi*	be, do, act as (3)
危		*wēi*	danger (7)
為		*wèi*	for (4)
未		*wèi*	not yet (3)
唯，惟		*wéi*	only (5)
謂		*wèi*	say, be called (3)
微		*wēi*	small, slight (8)
文		*wén*	pattern; writing; culture (6)
舞		*wǔ*	dance (9)
勿，無		*wù*	don't (5)
吾		*wú*	I, my (3)
霧		*wù*	mist (2)
誤		*wù*	mistake (10)
夕		*xī*	evening (9)
昔		*xī*	formerly (7)

戲	*xì*	play, joke (10)
習	*xí*	practice (5)
洗	*xǐ*	wash, bathe (10)
閑	*xián*	at leisure (3)
賢	*xián*	worthy (7)
相	*xiāng*	each other, one to another (5)
香	*xiāng*	fragrant (7)
向	*xiàng*	toward (9)
孝	*xiào*	filial piety (3)
小人	*xiǎorén*	petty person (2)
醒	*xǐng*	awake, sober (9)
性	*xìng*	inborn nature (5)
行	*xíng*	walk; take action, do (4)
休	*xiū*	cease, rest (8)
須	*xū*	need (8)
焉	*yān*	how; in it, by it, therefore, therefrom, etc. (6)
嚴	*yán*	strict, serious (7)
陽	*yáng*	light, creative principle (3)
藥	*yào*	medicine (8)
也	*yě*	final particle (3)
亦	*yì*	also (3)
異	*yì*	different (9)
醫	*yī*	doctor, heal (9)
矣	*yǐ*	final particle showing change of state (3)
依	*yī*	lean on, rely on, follow (6)
義	*yì*	righteousness, duty (3)
宜	*yí*	suitable (8)
以	*yǐ*	take, use, with (4)
陰	*yīn*	dark, nurturing principle (3)
飲	*yǐn*	drink (4)
勇	*yǒng*	brave (7)
永	*yǒng*	eternal (9)
猶	*yóu*	be like (3)
由	*yóu*	from, by (3)
於，于	*yú*	at, by, to, etc. (3)
與	*yǔ*	and, with; give (4)
予	*yú*	I (4)
餘	*yú*	more than; excess (5)
曰	*yuē*	to say, introducing a direct quote (2)
哉	*zāi*	final particle indicating question or exclamation (6)
則	*zé*	then (3)
賊	*zéi*	steal, thief (9)
戰	*zhàn*	war, battle (6)
朝	*zhāo*	morning (2)

照	*zhào*	shine on (3)
者	*zhě*	one who...; marker for topic (2)
至	*zhì*	arrive at, extreme, highest (3)
枝	*zhī*	branch (5)
致	*zhì*	extend, give (3)
指	*zhǐ*	finger, point to, refer to (3)
之	*zhī*	subordinating particle; him, her, it (2)
之	*zhī*	go (4)
志	*zhì*	goal, will, aspiration (2)
紙	*zhǐ*	paper (8)
止	*zhǐ*	stop, rest (3)
直	*zhí*	straight, direct (7)
智	*zhì*	wisdom, wise (7)
眾	*zhòng*	crowd, multitude (9)
舟	*zhōu*	boat (6)
諸	*zhū*	all; it + preposition (之 + 於) (6)
珠	*zhū*	bead, pearl (8)
主	*zhǔ*	lord, master; important; be in charge (7)
注	*zhù*	note, annotation (5)
住	*zhù*	stand, stop (7)
朱	*zhū*	vermilion, red (9)
子	*zǐ*	you (polite); Master (2)
自	*zì*	self; from (4)
足	*zú*	sufficient (5)
醉	*zuì*	drunk (9)

Contact China Books for our latest catalog of books from and about China including textbooks, reference books, dictionaries and computer software for learning Chinese.

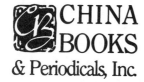 CHINA BOOKS & Periodicals, Inc.

2929 Twenty-Fourth Street
San Francisco, CA 94110
415.282.2994
FAX 415.282.0994